92 - Biog.
all

925

DATE DUE

NOV 25	3-13-96		
DEC 18	FEB 05 1997		
JAN 14	MAR 19 1997		
JAN 21	MAR 26 1999		
MAR 2	OC 11 '05		
DEC 22			
JAN 6			
FEB 9			
FEB 16			
MAY 3			
JAN 24			
FEB 26			
DEC 6			
JAN 9			
MAR 16			
PR 7			
APR 7			
MAR 07 1996			
GAYLORD			PRINTED IN U.S.A.

ALEXANDER THE GREAT

IMMORTALS OF HISTORY

ALEXANDER

Conqueror and Creator

Franklin Watts, Inc.
575 Lexington Avenue, New York 22

Charles Alexander Robinson, Jr.

THE GREAT

f a New World

First Printing
Library of Congress Catalog Card Number 63–16916
© Copyright 1963 by Franklin Watts, Inc.
Printed in the United States of America

To Celia

FOREWORD

THERE can be little doubt that the career of Alexander the Great had a more profound influence on the development of Western civilization than that of any other European in history. But, we may ask, did Alexander himself, in his own person, exhibit anything new and challenging? Was he an admirable man, or hateful? I am convinced that the youthful reader (for whom this biography is primarily intended) is eager to get the significance of Alexander and also to know how a historian determines the truth concerning a man who lived so long ago. I have therefore indicated in a general way the problems involved. They and their solution have their own peculiar fascination as well as value.

Like everyone else, Alexander had his contradictions, but because of his prominence, these have often been exaggerated beyond recognition. If we say, for example, that

anything written by an ancient Greek or Roman is holy
and correct, then it is possible to defend practically any picture of Alexander we like, because every kind of gossip
about him floated around in antiquity.

Most ancient Greeks hated Alexander because he destroyed the effectiveness of their city-state. Some distinguished modern scholars, such as George Grote, have been
carried away by their emotions and hate him for the same
reason. Other writers, not always familiar with the com-
plexity of our sources, have found it more convenient and
amusing to give the conventional picture of Alexander as
no more than a bloody conqueror, lucky despot, megalo-
maniac, and self-styled son of God. This picture is exciting
in a certain way, but it is worthless as history. Much of it
derives ultimately from the philosopher Aristotle whose
nephew, Callisthenes, was executed by Alexander, and
who hated the conqueror for this reason. The ancient
evidence yields a very different conclusion from that arrived at by Aristotle and those who have chosen him for
guide in their exploration of the truth about Alexander.

By far the best ancient biography of Alexander was
written by Arrian, a Greek of the second century A.D.
Another Greek, Plutarch, has also left a good account of
the man. Both Arrian and Plutarch are to be preferred, as
a rule, to Alexander's other ancient biographers, Justin and
Curtius, both of whom wrote in Latin, and Diodorus, a
Greek historian. All five of these writers lived three centuries and more after Alexander's death and obviously
knew nothing about him at firsthand. For their accounts,

the only consecutive ones we possess, they drew on earlier histories which now exist, if at all, only in fragments. Some of these histories were sound, some prejudiced. Arrian based his biography on the memoirs of two members of Alexander's expedition: one of these was Ptolemy, a general and future king of Egypt, the other was Aristobulus, an engineer.

Certain historians today have been able to demonstrate pretty well which of the surviving biographies and their sources are correct and which are false. It is our duty to be guided by the results of their specialized work. Those who would like to check my own interpretation by consulting the ancient texts will find precise references in my article, "The Extraordinary Ideas of Alexander the Great," *American Historical Review,* Vol. LXII, 1957, pp. 326–344; the modern literature on Alexander is indicated there. I should also call attention to W. W. Tarn's *Alexander the Great,* 2 vols., Cambridge, 1948, to which all students of Alexander are indebted. F. E. Adcock's *The Greek and Macedonian Art of War,* Berkeley, 1962, is a good introduction to the subject of warfare in Alexander's day.

I have used, with slight changes, Edward James Chinnock's translation of Arrian; Bernadotte Perrin's translation of Plutarch in the *Loeb Classical Library;* and Benjamin Ide Wheeler's translation of Curtius' description of the battle at Issus. I have Mrs. James J. Fine to thank once again for the typing of my manuscript.

C. A. Robinson, Jr.

Providence, Rhode Island

CONTENTS

ALEXANDER THE GREAT

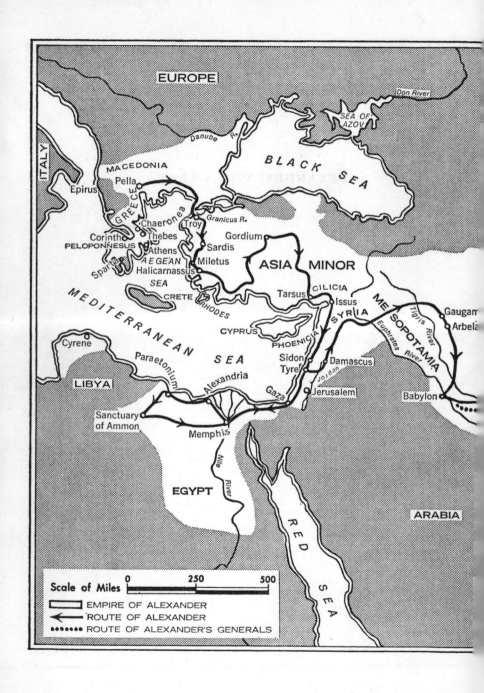

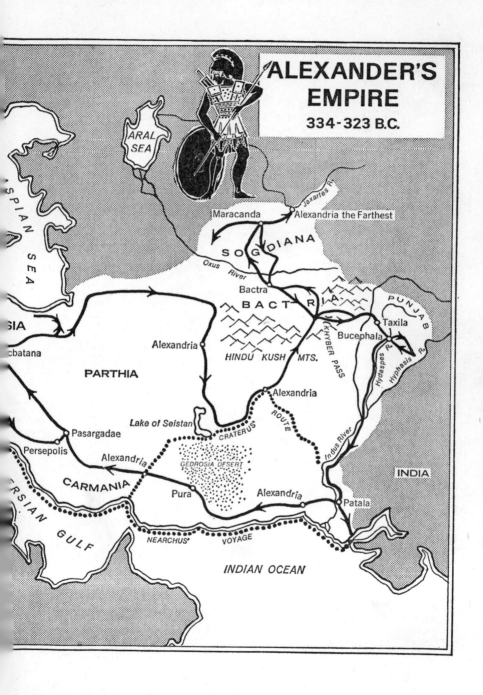

ALEXANDER'S EMPIRE
334-323 B.C.

ARAL SEA

CASPIAN SEA

Jaxartes R.

Maracanda

Alexandria the Farthest

SOGDIANA

Oxus River

Bactra

BACTRIA

PUNJAB

cbatana

SIA

PARTHIA

Alexandria

HINDU KUSH MTS.

KHYBER PASS

Taxila

Bucephala

Hydaspes R.

Hyphasis R.

Alexandria

Lake of Seistan

CRATERUS ROUTE

Pasargadae

Indus River

Persepolis

Alexandria

CARMANIA

GEDROSIA DESERT

Pura

Alexandria

INDIA

Patala

PERSIAN GULF

NEARCHUS' VOYAGE

INDIAN OCEAN

ALEXANDER'S YOUTH

Alexander the great was born in 356 B.C. Twenty years later he became King of Macedonia in northern Greece and went on to conquer the great Persian Empire. In 323 B.C. he died, not yet thirty-three years old.

Napoleon, who commanded a Grand Army himself, once remarked that Alexander was the greatest military genius in history, and that is the role the famous Macedonian conqueror has assumed in the minds of most people. But Alexander was far more than a military genius. He planned a universal society in which all people were to be equal, at least under certain conditions. This does indeed sound downright contradictory, for is it likely that a man would kill people by the tens of thousands and at the same time hope to unite humanity in the bonds of friendship? The fact is that Alexander's ideas could not have been born without his military triumphs.

Alexander died too soon to complete either his conquests or the administrative organization of his realm or his dreams for mankind. But he was successful enough in all three of these matters to change the course of history. As a result of his career, European, or Western, civilization ever afterward rested on that of classical antiquity. It is this that makes Alexander the most important European in history.

Alexander's life, after he became king, was one of continual military victories which, in turn, kept generating in him new ideas about mankind. He was not only a military but also an intellectual genius who conquered a world and, in the process, actually set the course which Western man has followed to this day.

Plutarch, the well-known Greek biographer of A.D. 100, says that Philip and Olympias, the parents of Alexander, met for the first time during their initiation into certain religious rites. Olympias was a fiery, passionate princess from Epirus—a section of Greece to the west of Philip's kingdom of Macedonia. During the ceremonies of initiation she led the women in a wild fashion, providing them with tame serpents, which would hide in the women's garlands and then suddenly dart out and terrify the men.

The story goes that Philip and Olympias fell in love with each other at sight and were soon married. The next summer, Alexander was born at Pella, the Macedonian capital. After Alexander became famous, it was inevitable that all kinds of stories should grow up about him and his parents. Few of the stories are literally true, but they have the value of showing what people believed or, at any rate, wished to believe. For example, not long after the wedding, Philip reportedly dreamed that he was putting a seal upon his wife's womb. The image engraved on the seal, so he thought, was the figure of a lion. Aristander, the chief court seer, declared that since no seal was put upon what was empty, the woman was pregnant, and pregnant of a son whose nature would be bold and lion-like.

It was also commonly believed in antiquity that the temple of Artemis at Ephesus, in Asia Minor, burned to the ground on the night of Alexander's birth. A contemporary historian made a remark, frigid enough to extinguish the flames, to the effect that it was little wonder that the temple had burned, since the goddess was busy bringing Alexander into the world. The Babylonian priests, known as Magi, who were at Ephesus at the time, looked on the temple's disaster as a sign of still more disaster to come, and ran about beating their faces and crying that the calamity of Asia had that day been born.

Philip himself was away from home at the time of Alexander's birth. He was off besieging the Greek city of Potidaea. On the very day that he took the city, he received three messages: that Parmenio, his best general, had conquered the Illyrians in battle; that his race horse had won a victory at the Olympic Games; and that Alexander had been born. The seers added to Philip's delight by saying that the son whose birth coincided with three Macedonian victories would always be victorious.

Such were Alexander's parents—a fiery visionary for mother, a king and coldly practical military commander for father. Quite naturally, Alexander inherited much from each parent. From his father he inherited military skill and a realistic approach to problems; from his mother, his ability to dream, his mysticism, and probably his temper, which was his worst enemy. It was from his mother, too, that the boy may have inherited the growing megalomania, or mania for greatness, that marked his later years.

According to common belief, there were various legendary ancestors in Alexander's background, and they were of the kind that might inspire a young man to tremendous exploits if the opportunity ever arose. Among these was Heracles, the Greek hero who had once performed twelve superhuman labors. Another legendary ancestor was Achilles, the greatest of the Greek warriors in the famous war against Troy.

In appearance, Alexander was of average height, fair complexion, and athletic build. Lysippus, Alexander's favorite sculptor, was said to have caught exactly the liquid and melting glance of the young man's eyes and the poise of his head, neck bent slightly to the left, a mannerism imitated by many of his friends and successors. Alexander's hair is said to have stood above his forehead like a lion's mane, and, unlike most of his contemporaries, he was beardless. For centuries men followed his habit of shaving clean.

Alexander's ambitions, even when he was a boy, were serious and somewhat haughty. When someone asked him if he intended to compete in the Olympic Games, since he was a swift runner, he replied, "Yes, if I can have kings as my competitors." On another occasion, when a remarkable horse named Bucephalus was offered to Philip for thirteen talents (roughly, $23,400), Alexander showed the courage and ingenuity that were to be so strongly manifest later in his life. The boy went down to the plain with his father to try the horse. The animal appeared wild and would not let anyone mount it. Philip ordered it led away, but Alexander exclaimed, "What a horse they are losing because they lack the skill to manage it!"

Philip asked his son if he thought he could do better than his elders, and Alexander said that he could. He even agreed to bet the price of the horse that he would succeed. Amid much laughter, he ran to Bucephalus and turned its head toward the sun, for he had noticed that the horse had been frightened by its own shadow. He then quietly mounted and, when he saw that the animal was ready for the course, urged it on.

Philip and those with him were speechless with anxiety at first, but when they saw Alexander make the turn in proper fashion and come back proud and exultant, they all cheered. Philip also shed tears of joy, according to eyewitnesses, and kissed his son when he dismounted. "My son," he said, "seek out a kingdom equal to yourself; Macedonia has not room for you."

The happy comradeship between father and son was frequently interrupted, however, by quarrels. Olympias, a jealous and sullen woman, did nothing to alleviate the quarrels. In fact, she spurred Alexander on.

The most open break between father and son occurred when Philip, who was at that time planning to attack Persia, divorced Olympias so that he might marry Cleopatra, a young niece of his general Attalus. Gossip had it that Philip had expressed doubt as to whether Alexander was really his son, and at the wedding banquet the bride's uncle, Attalus, called on the Macedonians to pray for a legitimate heir to the throne. Exasperated, Alexander threw a cup at Attalus, shouting, "Do you take me for a bastard?"

Philip thereupon drew his sword and made for Alexander, but he was so drunk and angry that he fell before he could reach him. Alexander mockingly shouted, "Look! Here is the man who was preparing to cross from Europe to Asia, and he is upset trying to pass from couch to couch!"

But this quarrel, like all the others between Alexander and his father, was eventually patched up.

Philip devoted very particular attention to the education of his son. The most important teacher he provided was, without any doubt, the famous and learned Greek philosopher, Aristotle. At the age of thirteen, and for three years thereafter, Alexander had the privilege of associating daily with one of the greatest intellects in history. He and Aristotle discussed philosophical, political, and ethical doctrines, among other things. During these discussions Alexander must have been exposed to Aristotle's belief that all foreigners, or barbarians (the Greek word for non-Greeks), were slaves by nature, especially the barbarians of Asia. This was indeed an extraordinary idea to suggest to a youth who would ultimately rule over a world of barbarians, and it will be enlightening to see how Alexander reacted to it.

The encyclopedic interest in Asia that Alexander later exhibited was, originally, at least, nurtured by Aristotle. This interest included medicine and natural phenomena, geography and peculiar plants.

Another result of the boy's long association with Aristotle was manifest during Alexander's long expedition in the East. There, in the midst of long marches and fierce fighting, he ordered many books to be sent him from Greece. Among these were the tragedies of Euripides, Sophocles, and Aeschylus. We are told that Aristotle made for his pupil a special edition of the *Iliad*, Homer's epic poem that sang the praises of Alexander's supposed ancestor Achilles, and that Alexander kept the book with his dagger under his pillow at night.

Alexander used to say that he admired Aristotle at first, and loved him more than he did his father, because the one had given him life, while the other had taught him a noble life. With the years, however, teacher and pupil grew apart; and in the long run, neither had much lasting influence on the other.

If courage, arrogance, and ingenuity had been Alexander's sole qualifications for leadership, he might still have turned out to be a great king. But Alexander, even as a boy, had a fourth quality that lifted him above the average, and that quality was intellectual curiosity. During one of Philip's many absences on a military expedition, for example, Alexander had the duty of entertaining envoys from Persia, the vast Asiatic empire he was born to conquer. He won over the envoys by his friendliness and by his restraint in not asking childish questions about the Hanging Gardens of Babylon or the dress of the Persian king. Instead, he inquired about the length of the roads, the warlike ability and courage of the king, and such matters, until finally one of the envoys exclaimed, "This boy is a great king! Ours is only wealthy."

II

MACEDONIA,
A MOUNTAIN KINGDOM

LIKE everyone else, Alexander was a product of his times and can be fully appreciated only in the light of them. The world of Macedonia, where he grew up, was quite different from the world of Old Greece, the Greece that had already made so many momentous contributions to civilization. The geography of Greece was not conducive to the development of a kingdom. Unlike the flat river valleys of Egypt and Mesopotamia, the rugged mountains offered no easy means of travel and communication. In the beginning, each Greek valley had its own political unit, a city-state that was theoretically, and often in fact, sovereign in its domestic and foreign affairs. Old Greece southward developed as a world

9

of city-states, each fiercely independent but always ready to encroach on the liberties of others.

In the century before Alexander, in that glorious fifth century B.C. which we associate with the name of Pericles, Athens had built an empire but had lost it in a long and terrible war with Sparta. In Alexander's century, the fourth before Christ, first Sparta and then Thebes tried, but failed, to unite the Greeks. War, political strife within the several city-states, a rampant individualism, an economic depression, and the steady interference of Persia in Greek affairs—these were some of the things that made men question past values. They questioned not only the worth of democracy, but also the ability of the city-state itself to give its citizens a full life. A people's loss of faith in its own institutions is a startling and disturbing thing to behold. The Greeks' loss of faith helps to explain their relative willingness to accept the arbitary rules of Philip and Alexander.

And so it happened that a kind of political vacuum had been created in Greece at a time when northward, in Macedonia, a vigorous new power threatened. Macedonia was not a collection of city-states but a nation, the first in European history. It had been fortunate in having a succession of kings who had united the land by a good system of roads and protected it by a standing army—a sharp contrast to the citizen militia of the Greek city-states.

The Macedonians, who were destined to conquer much of the civilized world, were a branch of the Greek people, but they were latecomers in history. Men in the ancient city-states looked down on them as uncivilized and even went so far as to say that they were really barbarians speaking a Greek dialect. When Philip became king, he did little to change popular Greek opinion, for the life in his northern mountain kingdom was relatively rough and crude. Philip himself drank heavily, quarreled incessantly with Olympias, who was doubtless a difficult person herself, and he had various love affairs.

But Philip was a man of many parts. During his youth he had spent several years as a hostage in Thebes where Epaminondas, the greatest general of his day, had inspired him to think along original lines in military matters. Here, too, in this ancient state, Philip had seen the glories of Greek civilization and had resolved to make Macedonia worthy of them. That is one reason why he ultimately chose Aristotle to tutor his son.

Many Greeks, among them the Athenian orator Aeschines, admired Philip. They saw, or thought they saw, the advantages of a monarchy, which could reach a decision more promptly than could a democracy. Union under such a state might bring prosperity to Greece. Moreover, some of Philip's admirers argued, why should the Greeks continue to kill one another when the hereditary enemy, Persia, might just as well be attacked and plundered? The Macedonian monarchy, they said, was precisely the instrument to unite Greece and bring about the defeat of Persia.

Most Greeks, however, continued to support the freedom and sovereignty of the city-states. The greatest of

Greek orators, the Athenian Demosthenes, urged the Greeks to unite against the northern menace. He attacked Philip in such biting language that similar speeches since then have been called "Philippics." Demosthenes pointed to Philip's growing military power, to the way Philip had lied and bribed opponents until at last Macedonia had become the most powerful state in Europe. Philip had recently seized Mount Pangaeus, with its valuable gold and silver mines. He controlled the crossing of the River Strymon and the road that led to Byzantium (Istanbul). His kingdom had outgrown the mountains of Macedonia and the strip of coast along the northern Aegean Sea. It now threatened all Greece.

III

THE GREEK CRISIS

THE fourth century B.C. was full of momentous and confusing questions. The issue before Greece, as some people saw it, was not just whether or not to take the patriotic course and oppose Macedonia. There were those who agreed with the Athenian orator, Isocrates, who insisted that federal union of the Greek city-states was the most pressing need of the day. These people rose above state boundaries and placed their emphasis on the human race, on universalism. They believed that peace and union, even under Philip, were preferable to constant warfare. Events, however, refused to wait for the Greeks to make up their minds. The issue was resolved for them by outsiders, by Philip and Alexander of Macedonia.

It was at Chaeronea in central Greece—the little Boeotian town where Plutarch was born four centuries later— that the future of the Greek city-state was irrevocably de- cided. The Greek allies, consisting chiefly of Athenians and Thebans, were thirty thousand strong, about equal in number to those with Philip. Philip had taken from the Theban general, Epaminondas, a tactical scheme which, like so much else, was to be further refined by Alexander. This particular scheme was, in fact, used by generals up to the time of Frederick the Great of Prussia. Essentially, it was to strike hard from one wing while holding the other wing firm.

In the past, it had been customary for a military com- mander to place his strongest forces opposite the weakest in the enemy's lines. In the beginning, at least, this was likely to create the illusion of victory. But Philip saw that it was better to defeat the enemy's best troops immedi- ately. Once the enemy's strongest wing was overwhelmed, it would be relatively easy to rout the remainder of his forces. And, as another contrast with the past, Philip did not limit his actions to the battlefield, but usually pursued the enemy as long as possible in the hope of wiping him out. Modern German writers on military affairs have called this "the strategy of defeat."

And so, at Chaeronea on a summer's day in 338 B.C., Philip stationed Alexander, now eighteen years of age, on the Macedonian left, directly opposite the famous Sacred Band of Thebans. Philip might have held firm on the Macedonian right, but the Athenians opposite him were on high ground, and so to deprive them of their favorable position, he pretended to retreat. Then he wheeled and

routed them, just as Alexander was rolling back and an-
nihilating the Theban forces.

The Macedonian victory was complete. It did not mean
that the city-state was dead, for it lived on as an ideal
and, in some places, as a reality, but never again was it the
driving force in Greek politics. The day of the large state
had arrived.

Philip had shown himself a master in battle; now he
was to prove himself a statesman as well. He called together at Corinth representatives of most of the Greek
city-states and formed them into a Panhellenic, or all-
Greek, union. This was called, after its meeting place, the
League of Corinth. The assembly of the League consisted
of representatives from the various Greek cities. Each city
was allowed to send a number of representatives corre-
sponding to its size. All decisions were to be carried out
by the Macedonian king, the League's military commander, or hegemon.

The League of Corinth was well designed to bring unity
to Greece, but not peace. Philip had other plans. Seizing
on the suggestions already made by Isocrates and other
Greek orators, he concealed his ambitions in a plea that
Persia be punished for its invasion of Greece at the opening
of the previous century. A Panhellenic war of revenge was,
therefore, to be the battle cry. Perhaps because it had no
real choice in the matter, the League voted that Greece and
Macedonia should undertake a joint expedition against
Persia. Philip himself would command the troops. His
own thoughts were doubtless concentrated on the wide
personal dominion that success would bring him.

IV

THE PERSIAN EMPIRE

THE Persian Empire, which was now to be attacked by Greece, was one of the most remarkable states in history. It had inherited from Assyria an excellent system of administration that assured distant provinces the same government as those nearer the capital. As a result, in the world from European Thrace to India there existed an internal peace and prosperity that were unique up to that moment. There is no denying, however, the autocratic nature of the government and its hereditary monarch, who was called "The Great King, King of Kings."

The Greeks looked on the Persian Empire as practically equivalent to the civilized world, for Italy and the West had not yet advanced very far on the international scene.

It was the East that counted in the thinking of men. Included within the Persian Empire were the ancient Greek cities along the Aegean coast of Asia Minor, such as Ephesus and Miletus, while the interior of Asia Minor was filled with a variety of peoples in different stages of civilization. Phoenicia, Syria, Palestine, Egypt, and Mesopotamia completed the empire's western flank. Just east and south of Mesopotamia was the homeland, Iran, or Persia, with the imperial capital at Persepolis. Eastward, the empire extended across modern Afghanistan and then northward over the Hindu Kush Mountains into eastern Iran—Bactria (northern Afghanistan) and Sogdiana (Russian Turkestan). Exactly how far east into India the empire reached we do not know, but certainly it included the Indus River and some of the plains (the Punjab) beyond.

The Persian invasion of Greece at the opening of the fifth century B.C., to which Philip had referred at Corinth, had ended in disaster for the invader; the victorious battles of Marathon, Thermopylae, and Salamis had become glorious Greek memories. As a result of the Persian defeat, the Greek cities of Asia Minor had won their freedom from Persia and joined the Athenian Empire. When Athens had lost her long war with Sparta at the end of the century, however, Persia had been able to reassert herself and incorporate the Greeks of Asia Minor once again in her empire. Ever since that time, Greek states and Persia had been meddling in one another's affairs, and now Philip had raised the cry of a war of revenge.

We have no way of knowing for certain, but probably his ambition ranged no further than Asia Minor.

Philip, however, seemed to be in no hurry to carry through his plans to invade Persia. He did send his experienced general, Parmenio, with ten thousand troops to seize the bridgeheads of the Hellespont, but he himself stayed in Macedonia. The two years following the battle of Chaeronea were mostly wasted in roisterous carousals, in quarrels with Olympias and Alexander, and finally in splendid preparations for the marriage of his daughter to the King of Epirus.

On the day of the wedding, distinguished representatives from the entire Greek world gathered in the theater of Aegae, the ancient Macedonian capital. The ceremony commenced at dawn with a long procession winding its way to the theater. Then came men carrying images of the twelve Olympian gods and, rather ominously, as people loved to say afterward, an effigy of Philip as the thirteenth god. But when Philip, all dressed in white, strode proudly forward, a Macedonian noble, who bore him a personal grudge, darted from the crowd and stabbed him to death (336 B.C.). Thus ended a life that had already altered the political map of Greece and promised further changes for a larger world. As Theopompus, a contemporary historian, put it, "Taken all in all, Europe has never yet produced such a man as Philip, the son of Amyntas."

Olympias seized the moment of Philip's death to kill his second wife, Cleopatra, together with her baby, by dragging them over a bronze vessel filled with fire. As for Alexander, it was, of course, one of the most difficult and critical moments in his life. He was only twenty years old; Philip had once doubted his legitimacy; and now, gathered together in the theater, were other possible successors to the throne as well as a number of famous generals. The deciding voice, Alexander knew, would be with the army, but even if it accepted him as king, what of the Greek states? He could not tell, not just now at any rate, whether they would remain in the League of Corinth and carry out the plan of war against Persia. These were the questions before Alexander.

The big question before the civilized world was what Alexander would do with his inheritance if he became King of Macedonia. If he did attack Persia, what really would be the point of it all? Would he have anything in mind except, like his father, to substitute Greek despotism for Oriental?

V

ALEXANDER—KING
AND HEGEMON

After his father's murder,
Alexander won the allegiance of the army and hence of
Macedonia. Now acclaimed King of Macedonia, he put
to death Philip's assassin, executed Attalus, Cleopatra's
uncle, for treasonable dealings with Athens, and received
pledges of loyalty from Philip's generals, Parmenio and
Antipater. Although we cannot read his thoughts, it is
clear from Alexander's actions that he intended to invade
the Persian Empire, for he promptly marched to Corinth
and convened the League. He then had himself appointed
hegemon, or commander in chief, of the Panhellenic war
of revenge.

Alexander now made two decisions that prove that he was intent on something far different from a mere marauding expedition into the Persian Empire. In the first place, he did not rush madly to the Hellespont and prepare his crossing into Asia. He spent the next two years in hard campaigning, north and west, so that when he did set out, his base in Macedonia and his flank would be secure. And, secondly, he brought with him to Asia a group of scientists and writers, as if to say that nothing less than permanent conquest was planned. This is not to suggest that Alexander certainly intended from the beginning to conquer the entire Persian Empire; rather, so far as we can tell, he put no limit on his plans and probably hoped to conquer a large part of the empire and then hold on to it.

If Alexander was lucky in having received from his father a strong kingdom, nothing could quite match his good fortune in inheriting the best military machine of the day. Now, as he secured his flanks, he took the opportunity to hammer that machine into an invincible force devoted to himself. Northward he marched, through trackless forests and over high mountain ranges, with wild tribesmen opposing him. His route led through modern Bulgaria to the Danube River. It hardly seems credible, but here in this wilderness he met his fleet, which he had ordered to sail from Byzantium into the Black Sea and then up the river.

Alexander was not planning to organize this part of the world. It was too uncivilized and unimportant for that. He merely wished to have the tribesmen see him and feel his power, so that they would not make trouble during his absence in the East. For the same reason he now crossed the river to the other side (modern Romania), subdued the tribes there, too, and then turned westward into what is modern Yugoslavia.

It was here that news reached Alexander that Thebes had revolted. If this great Greek city should succeed in asserting its independence, what would be the fate of Alexander's larger plans? With the speed that always distinguished him, Alexander moved his army through wild and unknown territory at the rate of twenty miles a day for two weeks. When he arrived at Thebes, he gave the people a chance to repent, and when they would not, he besieged and destroyed their city. This was Alexander's warning that during his expedition eastward, the rest of Greece must not abandon its obligations to the League of Corinth, to which it had recently renewed its allegiance. A very effective warning it proved to be.

In destroying the city of Thebes, Alexander spared the temples, and also the house and descendants of the famous poet Pindar. He did this not only to emphasize his respect for Greek civilization, but also to set himself off from the Persian invader who had ruthlessly destroyed Greek temples. In time, he regretted the destruction of Thebes. As various misfortunes befell him in Asia, he would say that Dionysus, god of wine and reputed grandson of the founder of Thebes, was taking vengeance on him.

Alexander's destruction of the ancient Greek city of Thebes was a great crime. It occurred at the outset of his career, and other crimes followed it until the end of his life. The historian, however, must strike a balance and see how a particular individual stacks up with others in this world of men. The destruction of cities was no more unusual in ancient days than it is in our own. Alexander's life of conquest, however, exhibits on the whole a humane treatment of cities and their populations.

Additional proof of Alexander's customary humanity comes from an unexpected quarter. Economic historians have studied the price of slaves during this period, and of course if the price had fallen as a result of Alexander's conquests, it would mean that he had regularly flooded the slave markets with the inhabitants of captured towns and cities. Nothing of the sort happened; and it is therefore well to remember antiquity's own verdict on Alexander, as represented by the words of Plutarch: "Alexander waged war according to usage and like a king."

It follows that, while we must never forget Alexander's crimes, we must also put them in their proper perspective. The verdict of the English writer Macaulay on Robert Clive (the victorious eighteenth-century British general in India) and on other men who are raised above the ordinary probably goes to the heart of the matter: "Their bad actions ought not, indeed, to be called good; but their good and bad actions ought to be fairly weighed." Accordingly, as we read about Alexander's exploits, we should, each of us, do our own weighing and pass judgment on the fundamental question: Does Alexander's life add up to anything more than another rattling good story of blood and thunder?

VI

THE OPPOSING ARMIES

THE care with which Alexander trained his army—by long marches north and west, by battles and sieges during his first two years as king— proved that he was not a reckless adventurer embarked on a gamble. At the least, he had an even chance against Persia, for this army of his had already defeated the Greeks at Chaeronea. During the past seventy years, moreover, several Greek expeditions that had penetrated the Persian Empire had met with partial success, showing that the imposing Persian Empire was far from invulnerable. What might not be accomplished by an expedition under a general more skillful than any who had preceded Alexander into Persia?

We must not suppose, however, that Alexander was about to come up against an unorganized or degenerate mass of so-called Orientals. The Persian Empire was civilized and ancient. Certainly it did not welcome Alexander, and just as certainly he upset a settled society. The Persian Empire was a mighty one, and it had kept peace within its own vast borders while it fought off intruders from outside.

The lands from European Thrace to India, a distance of three thousand miles, contained warriors of many different races. Not only his own sternly disciplined troops but also wild hillsmen and desert nomads were available to Darius III, the Great King of the Persian Empire. Warriors accustomed to many different ways of fighting awaited his command. In Asia Minor alone were stationed twenty thousand Persian cavalry, armed with javelins and reputed to be the best horsemen on earth. Darius also had at his disposal the equally famous Persian archers, a large body of Persian infantry, and twenty thousand Greek mercenaries, the envy of the world as foot soldiers. They could now be counted upon to take vengeance on the Macedonian conquerors of their homeland.

Although there is no doubt about the large size of the Persian military establishment, it is impossible to give the exact figures. Naturally, the Greek historians exaggerated the number of Persian troops in order to magnify Alexander's triumph in overwhelming them. We can understand, however, that the Persian commanders would take pride in their men and insist on formal battles with Alexander. Therein lay their chief mistake, for they were up against a true military genius and should have settled on a "scorched earth" policy and a plan of nibbling at Alexander's communications with Greece. Moreover, they should have tried to raise Greece in rebellion, for the Persian fleet was nothing less than the Phoenician navy, the best in the world, and the sea was theirs to sail.

Alexander also had a fleet, but a definitely inferior one, made up of Athenian ships which he had brought along really as hostages to assure the good behavior of the violet-crowned city while he was away. His strategy was to fight on land, and every mile of the way, except in Egypt, he was opposed. There were, perhaps, surprisingly few pitched battles—three with the Persians and another, his fiercest, with an Indian rajah. Here, for the first time, a European army met large numbers of elephants. It was a terrifying experience, since horses not trained to the smell of elephants are afraid of them. After Alexander's death, his successors engaged in mad efforts to obtain as many elephants as possible, but these generals were not of Alexander's caliber. Alexander himself used elephants in hunting and as transport, but never in battle, for he realized that a wounded beast is as likely to trample down friends as foes.

Alexander spent eleven years in Asia (334-323 B.C.). He marched thousands of miles, often at tremendous speed. He engaged in only four pitched battles, but most of the rest of the time was spent in fighting of some kind or other. Mountain tribes, hardy and wild though they might be, knew how to block passes, roll huge boulders down on advancing troops, fight in ordered fashion, and then disappear over the heights. Alexander developed the policy, whenever it was feasible, of attacking them in the winter, when snow would force them into the more accessible lowlands.

In addition to fighting the mountain tribes, Alexander had strong cities to besiege, deserts and jungles to overcome. In eastern Iran, a long and strange guerrilla warfare awaited him. On occasion, he was stricken with illness, and many a time he was wounded. Worst of all, he had to face disloyalty and even plots among his officers, few of whom could understand what he was doing. While the officers were thinking of a limited campaign, with its loot, Alexander seemed to be driving ever onward—where and why it was difficult to fathom. Sometimes Alexander was confronted with mutinies, not only of large bodies of troops, but of the entire army.

These were Alexander's chief problems. But in addition he had always to guard his communications and arrange for the regular arrival of reinforcements from home (more than sixty thousand troops reached him during the first eight years alone). Then, too, he had his empire to organize and administer—officials had to be chosen, a body of law must be decided upon, economic and physical health insured. And finally, he must formulate his new and extraordinary ideas for mankind, ideas that were sometimes offensive to his men. Taken together, this added up to a large program to be carried through during eleven years of constant warfare.

As a rule, Alexander's men were enthusiastically devoted to him. Perhaps this was inevitable, for Alexander was never anything but young, he was handsome and personally courageous, his expedition was the most dramatic in history and, of first importance no doubt, he never lost a battle. He also knew how to stimulate a vigorous rivalry between his various troops, to reward individual acts of bravery, and to spare and rest his men.

Alexander's army was a professional one, made up of Macedonian nobles and sturdy farmers who gave themselves over to years of service and training. Two things, in particular, help to explain its invincible power: first was Alexander's skill in building up a body of cavalry which could charge with such overwhelming force that it became his regular striking arm, something new in warfare; second—more difficult to achieve and requiring more imagination—was the combining of cavalry, infantry, and light-armed troops in all his actions, not only in the pitched battles but also in the smaller engagements, where a single detachment might be used. Alexander himself once ascribed his success to never putting anything off. Tactics, he said, meant using your brains, and certainly he was always ready to alter his tactics for a particular problem.

Those were the days when the commanding general usually fought in the front line with his men. Alexander was no exception to the rule, and in fact he was a conspicuous target for the enemy. His gleaming bronze helmet was crowned by a large crest with white plumes on either side; over his vest he wore a thick linen breastplate, and in his hand he carried a steel sword of exceptional temper and lightness. He usually rode Bucephalus in battle, until finally in India the horse died of old age.

The common situation in an ancient battle, until Alexander changed things, was for one mass of men to push another till one of them won. Alexander avoided this, holding back his personal body of cavalry until there was a break in the enemy's line; then he struck and struck hard at the opening, and from the flank rolled the enemy up. He had a special reason for making his right wing the offensive one. This was to protect the unshielded right side of his foot soldiers and keep them from unconsciously drifting to the right, which they were bound to do as each man sought the added safety of the shield on his neighbor's left arm. And, of course, Alexander's own charge would hit the enemy's left and accelerate its natural movement toward the right.

Alexander's famous phalanx consisted of 9,000 Macedonian foot soldiers, formed in tactical units of 256 men (sixteen men square). The extraordinary thing about these phalangites was their stiff training and discipline, which made it possible to keep a space of three feet between every two men. If they had been closer together —as greater protection might dictate—a dip in the ground or a sudden charge by the enemy would inevitably have toppled over a good many men unnecessarily. Now, however, the phalanx was flexible and could be easily maneuvered (which was also true, later in history, of the invincible Roman legion). The phalanx was generally formed as a rectangle, though it might be a square or something else. Here is a description from Arrian which shows how Alexander could occasionally win without fighting:

"Alexander ordered the foot soldiers first to hold their spears erect, then to couch them at the given signal; at one time to incline their spears to the right, closely locked together, and at another time toward the left. He then set the phalanx into quick motion forward and marched it toward the wings, now to the right and then to the left. After thus arranging and rearranging his lines many times very rapidly, he at last formed his phalanx into a sort of wedge, and led it toward the left against the enemy, who had long been amazed by the order and rapidity of his evolutions. Consequently, they did not sustain Alexander's charge, but withdrew." This was one way to spare your men; another was to induce a hostile city or area to surrender by the skillful use of propaganda, and in this, too, Alexander was a master.

The phalangite was heavily armed, with a bronze helmet, breastplate, greaves (shin guards), shield, sword, and a spear about thirteen feet long, weighted at the butt so that he could hold it several feet from the end. This was a far better weapon than the short sword in the hand of his Persian opponent. Alexander had other heavily armed foot soldiers and, with the phalangites, they occupied the center of the line in a pitched battle, acting as an anchor.

On the right wing stood Alexander and his magnificent horsemen, known as the Companion Cavalry. There were

2,000 of these heavily armed horsemen, wearing bronze helmets, breastplates, greaves, short swords, short thrusting-spears, and small round shields; stirrups and saddles belonged to a later century. The Companion Cavalry were divided into units of 250 men; as a rule, Alexander himself commanded a special group known as the Royal Squadron.

The cavalry on the left wing were under Philip's great general, Parmenio, the second in command. Parmenio was an older man, a cautious tactician, and therefore was admirably suited for the post: in this so-called oblique order of battle (which Frederick the Great also used) it was the duty of Parmenio and the left wing to hold firm, until Alexander at the decisive moment struck from the right.

Alexander had light-armed cavalry also. Some of these were placed to the left and right of his main wings, together with light-armed infantry, archers, slingers, and javelin-men. Finally, he had five thousand Greek mercenaries and seven thousand Greek allies from the League of Corinth: these latter were really held as hostages for the good behavior of Greece and, not being entirely reliable, were generally used for garrison duty.

The Grand Army, then, totaled something more than thirty thousand infantry and five thousand cavalry. At the top stood Alexander, King of Macedon and hegemon, commander in chief, of the League of Corinth. We must emphasize this dual role. An extraordinary fact about Alexander is the rapid evolution of his thinking, as rapid as his marches; thus, at the end of his life, he occupied so many different positions that it is impossible to describe him by any single title, such as King or Lord of Asia.

Among Alexander's chief generals and advisers were older men such as Parmenio, and also close personal friends: his bosom companion Hephaestion, and Nearchus, who was to be his admiral in the Indian Ocean. There were also Parmenio's son, Philotas, and Cleitus, who saved Alexander's life in battle, only to be murdered by Alexander in a drunken brawl. Others were Ptolemy, Seleucus, and Lysimachus, men destined to be powerful kings themselves, but who, during Alexander's life, were his obedient subordinates.

Alexander had an excellent intelligence corps, but long before he and his Grand Army reached India, he and his men were in a world totally unknown to their generation. It was the common belief that the "inhabited earth," the *oecumene,* was surrounded by Ocean. Alexander was at least vaguely familiar with Ocean's existence westward, for Greeks had been going past the Pillars of Hercules (Gibraltar) into the Atlantic. Then, at the Caspian Sea, he got the notion that he had reached a northern gulf of Ocean, and later on he was convinced that the Indian Ocean represented the southern limit of the earth. The eastern extremity, however, was a different matter, and became, for Alexander, a heartbreaking memory. It was his belief that Ocean lay not far east of the Indus River, but a mutiny of his troops stopped him short of his hoped-for goal. He remained completely ignorant of China and the subcontinent of India.

In the course of his expedition, Alexander was able to straighten out many of the current misconceptions about the earth, to the lasting benefit of Europe's geographical knowledge, for his innate curiosity did not exclude exploration.

Faulty as Alexander's knowledge of some parts of the world may have been, there was one thing of which he was almost never misinformed; namely, the details concerning the immediate terrain. In fact, his intelligence corps broke down only once, just before the battle of Issus. Similarly, his commissariat failed him only once, in the awful deserts of Gedrosia (Baluchistan).

Many men were needed by Alexander's army: cooks, attendants of the baggage train, and individuals who knew how to signal with trumpets, flags, and smoke when commands were not given by word of mouth. As a rule, ammunition and food were obtained from the countryside en route, but care was taken to protect the inhabitants from looting.

Most remarkable of all, because it was unique for the day, was the siege train. Military machines such as siege towers had, of course, been known in the past, but Alexander made his towers 150 feet high—so that they could be placed against any part of an enemy's wall and enable his men to jump across. He put the towers on wheels and protected them from fire by hides. Battering rams—great beams 100 feet long with metallic heads—and machines for tunneling under an enemy's walls were unlike anything in the past.

This important department of the army was under a Greek engineer named Diades. It was he, or someone in the army with him, who invented the torsion catapult— an engine resembling a huge crossbow—which could fire accurately for two hundred yards tremendous arrows, and stones weighing fifty or sixty pounds. In the early nineteenth century, it has been pointed out, a musket could not be counted on to hit its target at more than a hundred yards.

For some reason not wholly clear, Alexander never used catapults as artillery in a regular battle; rather, he used them in sieges and to drive an enemy away from the opposite bank of a river. It is easy for us to imagine the terror of wild tribesmen, shouting their insults at Alexander across a stream, when suddenly there landed in their midst some of these stones and flaming arrows. Needless to say, the tribesmen fled.

Excitement was at a high pitch in Macedonia in the spring of 334 B.C., for Alexander's Grand Army was now at its peak. Botanists, geographers, and other scientists were ready; so, too, were map makers, poets, and historians. Among the latter was a pompous Greek named Callisthenes, Aristotle's nephew, who once told Alexander that his fame depended not on what he did, but on what he, Callisthenes, happened to record; it was then that Alexander recalled the happier lot of his ancestor Achilles, who had Homer to describe his exploits.

It was the duty of Callisthenes to write a history of

the expedition on the march, and as he wrote he frequently checked his details against the *Ephemerides,* or Royal Journal. The Royal Journal was the official record of each day's events which Alexander ordered kept. This record became the basis of various contemporary histories of Alexander, such as those by Callisthenes, Ptolemy, and Aristobulus and hence was the ultimate source of Arrian, who wrote in the second century A.D. and who, as we have said, is our best surviving ancient biographer. As we ourselves draw on the ancient historians' use of the Royal Journal, we must remember that, primary source though it is, and as close to Alexander as we shall ever be able to get, it nevertheless represents the official truth; its relation to the real truth cannot be determined.

Olympias, like most women, did not go along on the expedition, but remained in Macedonia, constantly interfering in state affairs. Once, however, when Antipater, Alexander's regent in Macedonia, wrote a long letter criticizing her, Alexander said that Antipater did not realize that one tear of a mother outweighed ten thousand letters. Alexander had in Antipater just the man to represent his authority at home, for most Greeks did not support the expedition warmly and were ever ready to rebel. Moreover, Antipater must be applauded for his exceptional skill in regularly sending Alexander needed supplies and reinforcements.

As the day of Alexander's departure approached, and people began to realize the seriousness of it all, many omens and portents from heaven were reported. In particular, a wooden statue of Orpheus started to sweat, a sign that frightened most people. But Aristander, Alexander's chief seer, and a very useful one he was, announced that Alexander was about to perform labors that would cost poets much sweat to celebrate.

At the last moment, Parmenio suggested that Alexander should marry and have an heir, but Alexander brushed the idea aside. Instead, he said that since he had many debts he would give away most of his remaining property to his friends and then share his hopes with them. Thus it was, as farewell cheers rang out, that the Grand Army headed for Asia under a leader who was never to return.

VII

THE FIRST VICTORIES

ALEXANDER'S arrival at the Hellespont was pure drama. The narrow strait, which divides Europe and Asia and is now known as the Dardanelles, had seen masses of organized and unorganized men sweep across it in past ages, as they would continue to do in the centuries ahead, bent on conquest or loot or trade. Alexander knew that he was merely the most recent of predatory individuals to come this way, but if the thought sobered him, he gave no indication of it. Instead, he ostentatiously steered his own ship across, sacrificing to the gods in midstream, and on landing, set up altars to Zeus, Athena, and Heracles.

Because he loved adventure and had a sense of history, Alexander time and again did extraordinary things which appear to be mere stunts. Some of them doubtless were precisely that, but on closer examination others turn out to have been motivated by some coldly practical military

consideration. He had the ability, however, to dress up
his motive as a stunt and thus quietly to further his larger
design; perhaps we should expect this in the son of Philip
and Olympias. Now, for example, he did a most extraordinary thing.

Soon after landing in Asia, he dispatched Parmenio
and the main body of troops in the direction of the Granicus River, where the Persian army was known to be,
while he himself and some followers struck out for Troy.
In part, this was a reconnaissance action, to protect his
flank against possible Persian forces lurking in the neighborhood, but it was also and in large part a lark, a stunt.
After all, it would have been incredible not to visit the
city of Priam, which Homer had celebrated in his im-
mortal poems. A visit such as this, moreover, might be
made to pay large dividends. Nine centuries or so ago,
Agamemnon had led the Greeks this way, and Europe's
first famous invasion of Asia had ended in resounding
success. No Greek was unaware of this, because youths
during their schooling memorized as much of Homer as
they could.

Now Europe had another chance against Asia. This
was to be another Trojan War under a second Agamemnon, under a descendant of Achilles in fact, and surely it
was destined to as great success? If the visit was handled
with sufficient drama, it could stir a thousand memories
in every Greek and unite the faltering people at home
behind the new expedition.

At Troy Alexander anointed the gravestone of Achilles

with oil and ran a race by it with his companions, naked,
as was the custom. Then, while he placed garlands on
Achilles' grave, his intimate friend, Hephaestion, hung a
wreath on the grave of Patroclus, the bosom companion
of Achilles. Alexander then made libations to other heroes
and sacrifices to Athena, but there was little opportunity
for anything else. Time would tell whether the visit had
propaganda value. What mattered now, and in fact the
only thing that would ever matter, was to defeat the
Persians in battle.

Alexander, therefore, hurried back to his army and led
it to the Granicus River (May, 334 B.C.). The Persians
had taken their stand on the opposite side, where the banks
were steep and the stream narrow and swift. Important
provincial governors, or satraps, were present, as were
some of the chief generals of the empire, but not Darius.
The Great King had considered it beneath his dignity to
meet another contemptible intruder from Greece.

The Persian forces were large and included twenty
thousand cavalry and several thousand Greek mercenaries.
The mercenaries were under a very able Rhodian general
named Memnon, who now urged his Persian colleagues
not to fight Alexander in open battle, but to withdraw
and burn the countryside and its crops and even the cities.

The Persians turned down his advice with scorn. They
had their own plan of battle, and that was to kill Alexander at once and end the war. Therefore, they placed their
cavalry on the very edge of the river's bank, with the
infantry to their rear. This was an extraordinary error in

tactics, for the cavalry would have no space in which to charge.

This tactical error was immediately apparent to Alexander, and he ordered his army to line up for battle at once. Parmenio, ever the cautious tactician, said it was too late in the day to attack and that they should wait for the morrow. He pointed out that the Macedonians would have to go down into the swift river and climb up the steep and muddy banks under bombardment of multitudes of missiles, only to find at the top the ordered ranks of the Persians. But Alexander was unwilling to give the enemy a chance to reconsider its formations and told Parmenio that the Hellespont would blush for shame if he hesitated before this petty stream. It was typical of Alexander to give his men the sort of explanation they could readily understand.

Parmenio now took command of the left wing, Alexander of the right. For some time the two armies stood in silence at the river's edge, each afraid to precipitate the battle. Then suddenly Alexander charged. Many of his men were swept off their feet by the river's swift current, others floundered in the mud as they climbed up the steep bank opposite, some were killed by missiles, and those who got safely across and up the bank were attacked before they could form into any order.

The enemy, loudly shouting, pressed hard, and especially did they rush upon Alexander, who was conspicuous in his shining armor. First a javelin pierced the joint of his breastplate, and then two Persian generals made at him together. He broke his spear as he fought one of them, and took to his sword. Immediately the other Persian rode forward and, raising himself up on his horse, brought his battle-ax down with all his might on Alexander's head. Alexander's helmet stopped the ax just short of his scalp. While the Persian was raising his arm for another stroke, Cleitus, Alexander's friend from boyhood days, ran the attacker through with his spear, just as Alexander was killing his first assailant.

The battle was essentially a cavalry engagement, and by the time the Macedonian phalanx got across the river, the enemy had had enough. All but the Greek mercenaries had fled in rout. The mercenaries fought desperately and surrendered only when Alexander had reduced their ranks to two thousand.

Difficult as it is to recover ancient figures, especially those for the casualties, we do know that Alexander lost only two dozen members of his Companion Cavalry in his first onset. We know this because he ordered Lysippus, the famous sculptor, to make bronze statues of those who had fallen, and the statues were subsequently set up in Greece.

On the day after the battle, Alexander buried his dead and decreed that their parents and children should be exempt from taxes. He visited the wounded and let them boast about their exploits. He also buried those of the enemy who had fallen. To the Athenians he sent three hundred shields as a present, but to his mother he sent little personal things, such as Persian drinking vessels and purple robes.

The battle at the Granicus River was a decisive victory for Alexander and had ominous political implications for all Asia. For an understanding of Alexander's many-sided character, and his ability to develop his ideas rapidly on a variety of subjects, we should note that he sent the two thousand surviving Greek mercenaries back to Macedonia in chains, to till the soil. This was because they had fought for the Persians against an expedition that was, in nature, Panhellenic. Here Alexander was acting as hegemon of the League of Corinth.

Only a short time later, however, Alexander captured more Greek mercenaries, and instead of sending them back in fetters, he allowed them to enlist in his own army. We cannot say that in doing so he was breaking his connection with the League of Corinth, for the evidence shows that he found the League a convenient instrument to use from time to time. But it is clear that soon after his arrival in Asia he did not always take his position as hegemon seriously. It is too early in Alexander's career to place any label on his actions—much as we moderns love the easy convenience of such things—but it is fair to wonder if he was not aiming at outright personal dominion.

The Persians controlled the great Greek cities along the coast of Asia Minor through local tyrants. We have no way of really knowing whether or not Alexander believed in democracy, but he sensibly let the rumor spread that he had come to restore democratic government. In some places, such as Miletus, the propaganda failed, and he was held up briefly by the Persian garrison, but popular revolutions brought Ephesus and other cities into his camp at once. All these cities Alexander attached to himself as allies. When, soon afterward, he entered the district of Caria, he allowed the native queen, Ada, to adopt him as her son. Adoption of this sort was far more common in antiquity than it is today, and Alexander was happy to fall in with the suggestion. Now he could proclaim himself king of these barbarians—provided, of course, that they accepted his rule.

Alexander next disbanded his navy. He knew that it was inferior to the enemy's, and he realized that a defeat would damage morale out of all proportion to the defeat's true meaning. And now, because the mountains come down sharply into the sea, Alexander turned inland. It was a wise choice, for he could not go much farther east without safeguarding his flank.

As Alexander proceeded into the interior of Asia Minor, he collected taxes as though he were already the Great King. And in downright defiance of Aristotle's dictum concerning non-Greeks, he appointed "barbarians" as satraps of two provinces.

It was in the spring of 333 B.C. that Alexander reached Gordium. Reinforcements met him here, and so did the newly married young men in his army, whom he had considerately sent home to spend the winter with their wives. Enthusiasm was at a high peak, and Alexander saw to it that it stayed there. For example, there was a famous wagon on the Acropolis of Gordium, with the yoke fastened to it by a knot of cornel bark; anyone who could

untie the knot, so the story went, would become Lord
of Asia. For obvious reasons, Alexander had to undo that
knot, but when he examined it, he found that its ends
were very cleverly concealed. He therefore drew his sword
and cut through it (and ever since, those who have sum-
marily disposed of a difficulty have often been described
as "cutting the Gordian knot").

Alexander and his men were further pleased when,
that very night, there was much thunder and lightning,
the customary signs from the gods that their will had
been fulfilled. Better news, at least to Alexander, was the
report of Memnon's death. Darius had recently placed
the Rhodian general in command of the fleet, and a plan
had been evolved to raid Greece. The scheme evapora-
ted, and Alexander was able to set out against Darius
without worrying about his communications.

The halt at Gordium, to see a famous wagon, was
typical of Alexander's own romantic curiosity and of his
regard for the pleasure and relaxation of his men. The
ancient accounts speak time and again of the gymnastic,
literary, and musical contests he arranged for the army.
He himself enjoyed a leisurely day, too, whenever he
could. At such a time he sacrificed to the gods as soon
as he got up, and then had his breakfast. The rest of the
day he spent in hunting, or administering justice, or perhaps in reading or arranging military matters. If the army
was on the march, and the march was not very urgent,
he often practiced archery or mounting and dismounting
from a chariot. When he had established quarters for the

night and was taking his bath, he summoned his chief
cook and baker to make sure all the preparations for supper
had been made.

Late in the evening, when it was dark, Alexander had
supper with his friends. He took great care that everything should be properly served, and then, over the wine,
he and his friends would talk for a long time. This point
is emphatically made by the Royal Journal, by Plutarch,
and Arrian. It is not that Alexander did not occasionally
get drunk, for he did, but it was not a matter of habit.
In the evening, over the wine, he could relax with officers
and friends from boyhood days, learn what they were
thinking, and let them see him as they used to know him.
This renewing of old ties was important to Alexander, for
there is no denying that the responsibilities imposed by
large conquest were slowly isolating him from his friends.

Plutarch goes on to say that, although Alexander was
in other ways a most agreeable prince, he would become
boastful over the wine and allow himself to be influenced
by flatterers. When, finally, on one of these rare occasions
of leisure, supper was over, Alexander would take a second
bath and sometimes sleep until noon the next day—we
can hardly doubt that he was often in need of sleep.

Since the journey to Gordium had enabled Alexander
to make his power known in the interior of Asia Minor,
the task now was to come to grips with Darius. He must
move fast if he was to reach the coast of Cilicia easily, for
the route led through the Taurus Mountains, whose
main pass, known as the Cilician Gates, was very narrow

and could be held by a few defenders. Alexander marched at such a rapid pace that he got across the pass and even arrived at Tarsus before the Persians had time to make any effective resistance.

Hot and sweaty, Alexander plunged into the cold waters of the Cydnus River for a swim. Chill and fever followed, and his friend and physician, Philip of Acarnania, prepared a purgative draught. At that moment, however, Alexander received a letter from Parmenio in camp urging him to watch out for this Philip. Darius, Parmenio wrote, had persuaded the physician to kill Alexander, offering as a reward large sums of money and marriage to one of the ruler's daughters. Alexander put the letter under his pillow, without showing it to any of his friends. Then, when Philip came in with the medicine, Alexander gave him the letter to read. It was an amazing sight, says Plutarch, and well worthy of the stage, the one reading the letter, the other drinking the medicine, and then each turning his eyes on the other—but not with the same expression, for Alexander by his glad manner showed his confidence in his friend, while Philip was overcome by the false accusation.

Alexander recovered, and it is fair to guess that he recovered quickly, but the rumor spread that he would have to convalesce for a long time. Undoubtedly this was part of a scheme to entice Darius into the narrow Cilician plain where the huge Persian forces would have less advantage. In fact, Darius had already assembled a large army and was waiting for Alexander on the plains of northern Syria. Various advisers urged him to remain there, for Alexander's forces could be surrounded and annihilated in such a place, they said; but in the end Darius became impatient and said it did not suit his dignity to wait longer. And so he crossed Mt. Amanus from Syria into Cilicia.

Alexander, for his part, realized that he could not delay very long in Tarsus. After all, a conqueror must be ever successful, else the lands already conquered will rise in revolt. Thus it happened that Alexander crossed Mt. Amanus in search of Darius the very night that Darius crossed the same range by a different pass. It was the only time during his long expedition that Alexander's intelligence corps broke down. It failed him at a critical moment, too, for he woke up in the morning to find that the entire Persian Empire lay ahead of him, but that Darius and his army were behind him, between him and home.

Actually, the news was too good to be true, but scouts soon reported to Alexander that Darius was indeed in Cilicia, in the narrow plain of Issus, where the hills and sea would hem him in. Alexander immediately retraced his steps and on the dawn of a late October day in 333 B.C. reached Issus. Beyond the Pinarus River he could see the Persian dispositions.

According to custom, the Great King was in the center of the entire army, but he had placed his Greek mercenaries—perhaps 15,000 strong—in front of himself; as an extra precaution, he had ordered a stockade to be erected along the river's bank. Other infantry, and cavalry as well, spread out to his left and right, but on his left wing (in expectation of Alexander's charge from his own right) he had stationed the famous Persian archers. Altogether, Darius had an army that was larger than Alexander's; ancient accounts speak of 600,000 men, but the plain of Issus was too small for an army of that size, nor could the Persian Empire have produced so many troops.

Alexander probably still had 5,000 cavalry, though the infantry numbered considerably under the original 30,-000; reinforcements there had been, but many thousands had been left behind on garrison duty, and still others had been killed. Parmenio was sent to the left wing, with orders to hold the sea by all means. Alexander commanded the right, the phalanx was in the center.

At first, Alexander went from one body of troops to another and by appropriate speeches fired their spirits. Then he led his men forward slowly until the arrows of the Persians began to reach them. This was the moment to charge, and so rapidly did Alexander move that the Persian left was quickly rolled back. Now he turned against the Persian center where, in the rhetorical account of Curtius, he did "the work of a soldier no less than that of a leader. For there stood Darius towering aloft in his chariot, a sight that prompted friends to shield him and foes to assail him. So then his brother Oxathres, when he saw Alexander rushing toward him, gathered the horsemen of his command and threw them in the very front of the chariot of the king. Conspicuous above all the rest, with his armor and giant frame, fighting now the battle of his life, Oxathres laid low those who recklessly surged against him.

"But the Macedonians grouped about Alexander, heartened by one another's exhortations, burst in upon the line. Then came the desolation of ruin. Around the chariot of Darius you would see lying leaders of highest rank, perished in a glorious death, all prone upon their faces, just as they had fallen in their struggle, wounds all in the front. Among them you would find famous satraps and great generals; piled up around them a mass of footmen and horsemen of meaner fame. Of the Macedonians, too, many were slain, good men and true. Alexander himself was wounded in the right thigh with a sword. And now the horses attached to Darius' chariot, pricked with spears and infuriated with pain, tossed the yoke on their necks and threatened to throw Darius from the car. Then he, in fear lest he should fall alive into the hands of the enemy," turned and fled, coward and despot that he was.

Alexander had to delay pursuit because the Greek mercenaries were giving his phalanx a rough time, and the Persian cavalry had even crossed the river and were pressing Parmenio back. Gradually, however, word of Darius' flight spread throughout his troops, until at last they all fled, each man as best he could. Alexander immediately went after Darius and pursued him with all his might as long as it was daylight. According to Arrian, Ptolemy recorded in his memoirs that they actually crossed a gully on the bodies of the dead. Nightfall, however, saved

Darius. He had fled in his chariot, but when he came to uneven ground, he took to his horse, abandoning his chariot and even his shield, bow, and mantle. Alexander brought these back to his camp as trophies.

On his return to Issus, says Plutarch, Alexander found that his men had picked out for him the tent of Darius, which was full of beautiful furniture and other treasures. Alexander at once took off his armor and went to the bath, saying, "Let us go and wash off the sweat of the battle in the bath of Darius." "Not at all," said a friend, "but in the bath of Alexander, for the property of the conquered belongs to the conqueror." And when Alexander saw the tubs and pitchers and caskets, all of gold and wonderfully wrought, while the apartment itself was marvelously fragrant with spices and unguents, and as he passed from one huge tent to another, and found a banquet already prepared for him, he turned to his friends and said, "This, it seems, is to be a king." Certainly it was all a sharp contrast to his simple Macedonian home.

As Alexander went off to supper, word was brought him that among the prisoners were the mother, wife, and two unmarried daughters of Darius. They had seen his captured chariot and bow and were now lamenting him as if he were dead. After a moment's thought, Alexander sent a message to them saying that Darius was alive and that they would have all the comforts they had been accustomed to, for he was making war on Darius and only on Darius. Alexander treated them royally.

Years later, to legitimize his rule, Alexander married

one of Darius' daughters, but he never laid eyes on Darius'
wife, whom the Macedonians considered the most beautiful woman in Asia. Darius' daughter was Alexander's
second wife, for even earlier he had married Roxane,
daughter of a powerful Iranian baron. His first marriage
was also a political match, but from it, after Alexander's
death, was born a son and heir. Twelve years later, the
boy and his mother were both murdered by a Macedonian
general.

Alexander, according to the reliable ancient accounts,
never had a mistress. This probably means that he was not
notorious in such matters, and certainly we can say that
he was far too busy to spend much time with women.
Plutarch says that, though Alexander was impetuous
and often violent, the pleasures of the body had little hold
on him and he indulged in them with great moderation.

On the day after his triumphant battle with the Persians, Alexander visited the wounded, gave gifts to those
who had been especially brave, erected altars of thanksgiving to the gods, and, in a magnificent ceremony, buried
the dead. Despite the fact that we have the eyewitness
accounts of Callisthenes and Ptolemy for the battle of
Issus, it is a little difficult to believe that Alexander lost only
450 men; we cannot even guess the Persian losses, though
they were surely very large, as is always the case in a defeated army.

Only a year and a half had passed since Alexander
crossed the Hellespont. During that time, he had won two
pitched battles with the Persians, had cleared their gar-

risons out of the coastal cities of Asia Minor, had brought
the interior over to his rule, and had subdued innumerable
hill tribes. He had treated captured Greek mercenaries as
he wished, sending some back to Macedonia in chains and
allowing others to enlist in his army. To promote economic prosperity, Alexander also began great public
works, notably the rebuilding of the temple of Artemis at
Ephesus, which had burned down on the night of his
birth.

During these crowded eighteen months, moreover,
Alexander had restored democratic government in most of
the cities. The administration of the entire conquered area
—in size, not much smaller than modern Turkey—had
been organized. Under the Persians, it had been customary to concentrate tremendous power in the hands of
the provincial satrap, but in the interest of the governed
Alexander now started a separation of authority, ultimately assigning military, civil, and financial functions to
different individuals. Whether he would ever be able to
give a sense of unity to his state, only the future could
tell. No empire in the past had even aimed at such a goal,
and perhaps it was not in Alexander's mind at that time.
The appointment of two barbarians as satraps points in
that direction, however, for Asia Minor was a world of
Greeks and it would have been both easy and natural to
rely on them to govern. Finally, although he had entered
Asia Minor as King of Macedon and hegemon of the
League of Corinth, Alexander became in addition the ally
of the Greek cities along the coast and the adopted son of

a native queen. As he passed through the interior of Asia Minor, he posed as the Great King.

It is still too early in Alexander's career to say what position he proposed to occupy in his realm. Probably he did not know himself. It is clear, however, that he was taking over the different forms of government as he came upon them in an ancient and varied world. This would inevitably mean that he would have a different title and status in the various sections of his empire, but no matter what title he claimed, all areas were to be under his rule.

At the moment, the Persian Empire stood, and Darius, though in flight, was still alive. The battle of Issus, however, meant that Asiatic power in the eastern Mediterranean was finished: that vast area was to be ruled by Europeans throughout the rest of antiquity. But in coming this far, past the Greek cities of the coast to the very edge of Syria, Alexander had doubtless conquered more than Philip had ever planned, or the Greeks at home thought necessary. Most people were probably wondering whether Alexander would call a halt at this point or pursue Darius before the Persian could re-form his armies. Alexander did neither.

VIII

TYRE AND EGYPT

T HE idea of bringing his expedition to an end with the conquest of Asia Minor apparently never entered Alexander's head. Soon after Issus, he sent Parmenio to Damascus to seize the Persian treasures that had been left there, while he himself immediately and automatically turned down the Mediterranean coast. A lesser general might easily have decided that pursuit of Darius was the obvious plan to follow, but against this could be set other considerations. First and foremost was the fact that the Persians' Phoenician fleet had recently moved into the Aegean Sea, with the intention, surely, of raiding Greece.

Since Alexander had been willing to spend his first two years as king in marches north and west to protect his flank, and since his communications with Greece had been constantly on his mind from the outset of his expedition, it is not surprising that he gave priority to such things now. In general, he reasoned, it would be best to continue down the Phoenician coast and even to Egypt and then, with the entire eastern Mediterranean in his possession, to seek out Darius. If the enemy held the coast, it would be extremely dangerous for Alexander to march farther east into Asia.

The task of putting the Phoenician fleet out of commission, at least as a hostile force, was not as much of a problem as it would first appear. To be sure, Alexander had no navy of his own, but he was sure that if he captured the Phoenician cities, if he held the homes and bases of the Phoenician fleet, the crews would desert to him. He was not far wrong in his reasoning. And as he marched down the coast, one city after another surrendered.

Tyre proved to be something else, however. It wanted neither Macedonians nor Persians, and could remember how it had once successfully withstood a thirteen-year siege by the Babylonian king, Nebuchadrezzar. Tyre's strength lay primarily in the fact that it was an island, half a mile offshore, and fortified strongly by stone walls. The Tyrians could also count on their excellent navy and on their military machines, some of which were extraordinarily novel.

A siege of seven months awaited Alexander; the capture of the famous commercial city, the founding mother of Carthage (Rome's terrible North African enemy in the next century), was to be his greatest military exploit.

First, however, there was diplomatic jockeying. The Tyrians sent envoys to surrender their city, by which they meant the Tyrian settlement on the mainland. Alexander thanked them and suavely replied that he would like also to visit the island and sacrifice at the shrine of the Semitic god Melkart, who was known in Greece as Heracles, his own ancestor. The Tyrians pointed out that Alexander would do better to remain on the mainland and do his sacrificing there, since its shrine was even older than that on the island. And so the siege commenced.

The number of omens and portents that were reported by both sides revealed the intensity of feeling, the fears and hopes, and the determination of the contestants. Alexander, for instance, announced that he had dreamed that Heracles had led him into the city. Aristander, ever the helpful seer, said this meant that Tyre would be taken only after great labor, since the achievements of Heracles were accomplished by labor. And on their side, many Tyrians dreamed that Apollo was leaving them for Alexander. Thereupon, they tied the god's statue and nailed it to the pedestal, as if Apollo had been a common deserter caught in the act of going over to the enemy.

As soon as he decided to attack the city, Alexander began to build a mole, two hundred feet wide, from the mainland to the island. He kept the enthusiasm of the men at a peak by working hard himself and from time to time making appropriate speeches and rewarding outstanding performance with gifts of money. At first, the work went well, for the water was shallow near the shore, and the men were out of range of the Tyrian military machines. But as Alexander and his men approached the island city, the water was eighteen feet deep, and the Tyrians were able to hit the Macedonians with their missiles. Furthermore, the Tyrian triremes kept up a running attack on the mole. (A trireme was the conventional ancient warship and took its name from the fact that it was propelled by three squads—not banks—of about 60 oarsmen each; it was approximately 120 feet long, 20 feet broad, with a heavy metallic ram in front, and it carried marines.)

To protect themselves, the Macedonians erected two towers on the mole, covered them with skins against flaming arrows, and set up catapults to shoot back at the triremes. The Tyrians then filled a large ship with dry wood, pitch, and brimstone, and hung from the yardarms of the two masts caldrons of other inflammable matter; they weighted the stern down, so that the bow would be lifted high out of the water. Then, when the wind was right, they set the ship on fire and ran it on the mole. As the masts burned, the caldrons dumped their inflammable material and added it to the blazing mole and its towers. Alexander immediately ordered another mole built, broader than the first, so that it could hold more towers. Eventually this mole became covered with silt, so that today Tyre is part of the mainland.

Alexander now realized that he must have triremes himself, and accordingly he marched back to Sidon and other Phoenician cities with a contingent of troops. News of Darius' defeat at Issus had spread far and wide by now

and, as Alexander had expected they would do, 80 Phoenician triremes and 120 from Cyprus deserted to him.
Then, to obtain some of the famous cedars of Lebanon for
building still more ships, he went up into the mountains.

It was during this expedition that Alexander risked his
life to save Lysimachus, one of the tutors of his youth. The
way up the mountain was steep, and the two men were on
foot. Most of the Macedonians had got far ahead, but
Alexander was unwilling to abandon the old and weary
Lysimachus, even when darkness fell. The night was very
cold, and in the distance Alexander could see the scattered
fires of the enemy. He ran to the nearest campfire, stabbed
the two men he found there and then, snatching up a
firebrand, brought it back to his own little party. With
this they built a large fire and frightened off the enemy.
These little acts of devotion to friends, and his willingness
to share the toils of others probably won Alexander as
much popularity with his men as did his personal bravery
in battle; certainly he seems generally to have been con-
scious of the necessity of setting a proper example.

When, at last, a respectable fleet had been gathered together for him at Sidon, Alexander went on board with
some of his troops and set sail for Tyre. The Tyrians were
amazed to find that they were no longer supreme at sea
and, refusing battle, blockaded their two ports, the one
facing toward Sidon and the other south toward Egypt.
At the same time, they strengthened their walls, raising
the wall opposite the mole to a height of 150 feet. This
wall consisted of huge blocks of stone set in cement, and

was consequently very broad. When it was finished, the Tyrians rolled tremendous boulders into the sea so that the enemy's ships could not get too close to the walls.

The question now before Alexander was how to move his engines up to the walls, either by ship or along the mole, which was now almost finished. Before moving the engines by ship, he had to drag the boulders away by boat, and the Tyrians sent divers to cut the rope cables of his anchors. Alexander then used chains as cables, and by means of cranes dropped the boulders into deep water.

The way was now clear for a direct assault on the walls. Bridges were thrown across, now here, now there. But as the Macedonians attacked, the Tyrians threw nets over the men and dragged them down; still others they plucked off with iron instruments called crows. Moreover, they were able to put battering rams out of commission by cutting the cords with sharp hooks fastened to long poles. They heated large pieces of iron and shot them at the Macedonians; they dumped sand, scorching hot, on them, and of course it got inside their breastplates and burned their flesh. Then the Tyrians made the terrible mistake of bringing some Macedonian prisoners to the top of the wall and, in the sight of all, slaughtering them and casting their bodies into the sea. This, no less than the length of the siege itself, gave Alexander and his men an excuse for the massacre that soon followed.

Arrian says that, as soon as part of the Tyrian wall had been knocked down, "Alexander ordered some triremes to sail against the two harbors and others to run aground and

begin shooting at the Tyrians, so that they might be shot
at from all sides and not know where to turn. Then, as
bridges were thrown from still other ships, heavy-armed
Macedonian infantry crossed to the wall, led by Admetus.
Alexander went with them, both as a courageous partici-
pant in the action itself and as a witness of dangerous feats
of valor performed by others. Admetus was the first to
mount the wall but, while cheering on his men, he was
struck by a spear and died on the spot. Finally, Alexander
and his men took the wall and advanced into the city
against the main body of the Tyrians, who had rallied at
the sanctuary of Agenor, and routed them. A great slaughter was also made by those who had forced the harbors.
About eight thousand Tyrians were now killed; and of
the Macedonians, besides Admetus, twenty died in the
initial assault that day, and about four hundred in the
entire siege." The rest of the Tyrians—thirty thousand or
more—were sold into slavery (July, 332 B.C.), the first
of the three occasions known to us when Alexander sold
captives.

The capture of Tyre was necessary to Alexander, for the
march to Egypt could not be resumed until this strong
naval base had fallen. But its destruction and the treatment of its people can only be described as a very great
crime, one that must be put into the scales for the final
weighing of Alexander's character and significance. Certainly he was relentless and single-minded in his determination to win his goal. Exactly what that goal was could
not yet have been entirely clear to him, but his adminis-

trative arrangements for Asia Minor prove that he was thinking along extraordinary and novel lines: a new society of some kind was in the making. Few people tried to understand him, for the chief thing in *their* minds was the opportunity for loot. Thus there developed, slowly but surely, a chasm between Alexander and his men.

The point is illustrated by the story of a letter which Alexander received from Darius during the siege of Tyre. As ransom for his family, Darius offered Alexander 10,-000 talents (one talent = ca. $1,800) together with all the lands west of the Euphrates River, a daughter in marriage, and alliance. When Alexander discussed the subject with his friends, Parmenio remarked, "If I were Alexander, I would accept these terms and put an end to the war." "And so indeed would I," replied Alexander, "were I Parmenio." He then told his friends that one more battle with Darius would be necessary, after which they would have peace. Once again, as before the battle of the Granicus, he gave the explanation that could be readily understood—that he intended to have the entire Persian Empire; other matters he kept pretty much to himself.

The way to Egypt was not yet open, however, for the Arabs in the city of Gaza refused to submit. During the desperate siege, a shot from a catapult went right through Alexander's shield and breastplate into his shoulder; the fighting on both sides was intense, until at last the city was taken amid slaughter that almost defies description. The details of Gaza's destruction rest on contradictory and unsatisfactory evidence, but it is clear that Alexander was not always the master of his temper. Like Tyre, Gaza, at last captured, was turned into a Macedonian fortress.

After so much fighting, it must have been a welcome change to reach Egypt (November, 332 B.C.), for the Egyptians had long chafed under the Persian misrule and went over to Alexander without striking a blow. For centuries, Egyptians and Greeks had known each other, cultural influences had passed back and forth, and traders had exchanged their wares. Herodotus, the Greek historian of the fifth century B.C., had visited Egypt and had included in his historical account various fascinating tidbits about the land: how to embalm a body, how to catch crocodiles, how to build a pyramid, and so on. The wonders of this ancient civilization must have struck the members of the Grand Army with awe, not least of all the religious practices, for Greeks were ever ready to seek the benefits of another religion.

There was nothing unusual, however, in the fact that the Egyptians greeted Alexander on his arrival as the son of Ammon, for it was their realistic habit to regard every Pharaoh, or ruler, as the son of their great god. It did, of course, legalize Alexander's position as ruler, but it had no other significance in Egypt and none whatsover elsewhere.

The truly important thing that Alexander did in Egypt was to found a city that soon grew to include a million inhabitants and has remained ever since one of the busy seaports of the Mediterranean. This was Alexandria, named after himself; it was placed west of the westernmost mouth of the Nile and therefore, thanks to the currents of the

Mediterranean, it was free from the silt of the river. In all their centuries, the Egyptians had not discovered this secret and had never built a great city on the coast. Very probably Alexander was able to choose the site so speedily because of the scientists he had with him.

This was not the first time that Alexander had founded a city, and the years ahead were to see many more Alexandrias. In the farther East, where there were few cities, Alexander's foundations were often brand new, but as a rule the foundations which he scattered across Asia (reputedly seventy in number) were not new. They represented, rather, the addition of colonists to existing communities. The settlers were chiefly Alexander's soldiers who, because of age or wounds, were no longer useful as active fighters. The new "cities" were placed at strategic points, so that they could police the neighborhood and protect supplies and reinforcements as they came along.

Alexandria beside the Nile satisfied several requirements. Now that Alexander held the entire eastern Mediterranean, the city might become the capital of his empire, unless, of course, he succeeded in his larger designs against Darius; in that case, Alexandria would at least become a great administrative seat. Then, too, the destruction of Tyre made it necessary to create some other commercial center for that part of the world. Long ago, the Egyptian Pharaohs had connected the Red Sea and the Nile by a canal (the Suez Canal goes directly from the Red Sea to the Mediterranean). The canal had silted up during the Persian occupation, but its significance was not lost on

Alexander: here, in all probability, was a direct connection by sea with India.

In one way or another, Alexander was being constantly reminded of large vistas and opportunities before him. If a new kind of society, or state, was actually within his grasp, vigorous trade would be necessary to provide a wonderful prosperity, and in this regard Alexandria was well situated to serve as a link between East and West. A far more difficult task would be to give his state a common idea or ideal, to provide a unifying force in an empire that already included many different peoples. What could possibly be the cement of this empire? Alexander eventually solved the problem by creating a new attitude toward the world.

It took some years to work this out, but Alexandria was a conspicuous beginning in a special way. The fact is that Alexandria beside the Nile and all those other foundations of the future were something more than military, administrative, and economic centers. They were also places full of Greek and Macedonian soldiers, who inevitably would hold forth to the barbarian world round about them the ways of the Greeks, Greek law and art and life. A common culture for mankind might become the driving force of Alexander's empire, and since he had no doubt concerning the superiority of Greek civilization, Alexander guessed—it could not have been much more than that at first—that from these new foundations would spread the germs of a common Hellenic civilization. The idea steadily developed in his mind, along with other strange thoughts.

In the final issue, the Hellenization of Hither Asia came about in just this way, and there can be no doubt that this was the most important concrete result of Alexander's life.

Alexandria was exceptionally well situated to become a busy port. The island of Pharos protected the harbor (later, a successor of Alexander built a lighthouse on the island, four hundred feet high, which was adjudged one of the seven wonders of the world); a mole was built connecting the island with the city, and to the rear of it were a lake and an inner harbor. Needless to say, when Alexander ordered sacrifices to be made, all omens favored the project.

Alexander left his army at work on the new city and, with a few followers, took a trip that eventually wound up in the Libyan desert, at the Oasis of Siwah, as it is called today. Here was located the oracle of Zeus Ammon, in Greek eyes one of the most important oracles in the world, second only to that of Apollo at Delphi. There were several reasons why this oracle should have been so highly regarded by the Greeks; for one thing, it was far off from Greece, and the grass on the other side of the fence has always seemed greener. For another, its setting in a desert oasis was extraordinary, its connection with Egypt was fascinating, and the chief gods of the Greeks and the Egyptians were here united in one.

Nothing that Alexander ever did has led to so many stories as this trip of his. Since few of these stories are true, let us first set straight the facts of history. The usual, direct way to go to the oracle was right across the desert from

Memphis (modern Cairo, near the great pyramids). Alexander, however, went first along the coast, and a glance at the map will show far to the west the important Greek city of Cyrene, one of the few cities the Greeks had been able to found in Africa, because of Phoenician competition. Alexander's trip, then, was another example of military reconnaissance; he wanted to make certain that an attack on Egypt would not be delivered from the flank while he pursued Darius. We have the precise statement of two ancient historians, Diodorus and Curtius, that Alexander kept going along the coast until envoys from Cyrene met him and offered him the city's submission.

That was enough. Alexander immediately left the coast for the desert. Military considerations were at work here, too. It was best to make certain that the Libyan desert actually existed as a bulwark for Egypt, and then to bribe the priests at the oasis to police the area for him. But the trip could also be full of thrills for a highly adventurous young man. There was, for instance, the challenge of the desert itself, which had once overwhelmed an army with the Persian king, Cambyses. What a Persian had once attempted, Alexander must surely accomplish! The desert journey would be difficult, but at the end was the oracle, famous in Greece, and for Alexander's romantic nature, especially alluring. His own ancestors, Perseus and Heracles, reputedly had once consulted it; and he, who in his first year as king had already consulted the oracle at Delphi, must now by all means visit that of Ammon.

And so the journey across the sands commenced.

Arrian, getting his facts from the memoirs of Ptolemy (who accompanied Alexander on the trip), says that "they lost their way, as even the guides were in doubt about the course to take. Ptolemy says that two serpents went in front, uttering a voice, and Alexander ordered the guides to follow them, trusting in the divine portent." In any event, the oasis was reached. Alexander was struck with wonder at the place and went into the inner shrine alone with the priest. "Having heard what was agreeable to his wishes, as he himself said," Arrian concludes, "Alexander returned to Egypt," directly across the desert to Memphis. That is all that Arrian tells us about Alexander and the priest, and therefore it is all that we shall ever know.

There is really no reason for us to expect more, because the visit with the priest had been a spree, it was now done and finished, and years were to pass before Alexander referred to it again. If anything else had passed between Alexander and the priest—especially if it had touched on Alexander's origin—we may be sure that Ptolemy would have mentioned it: it would have made excellent propaganda for himself as Alexander's successor and king of Egypt.

To understand Alexander fully, however, we must bear in mind that he was already famous, with ever more extraordinary feats just ahead of him. Mankind has always loved to surround such men with apocryphal stories, and while they cannot be used as evidence for the individual himself, they do tell us what people wanted to think about

him. Alexander, in fact, moved the imagination of posterity as few have ever done, and ultimately the trip to the
oracle of Ammon was turned into the fanciful tale that he
had gone with the intention of being saluted as the son of
God. The story began simply enough, with a slip in pro-
nunciation by the priest. According to Plutarch, the priest
meant to address Alexander with the friendly greeting,
"O paidion," or *O my son,* but, being a foreigner, he
made a mistake with the final letter of the Greek and said,
"O paidios," which could be divided into, "O pai Dios,"
or *O son of Zeus.*

There were bound to be stories, too, about the parents
of this complex and famous man. We may recall, for
example, that Philip once told Olympias he was not sure
he was Alexander's father. It was easy, later on, to read
something special into this remark, particularly as it could
be connected with another story. Philip once lost an eye in
battle, and in time the story circulated that the oracle at
Delphi had actually prophesied that he *would* lose it, not
because of bravery, however, but because he had dared to
peek through the keyhole one night when Zeus, in the
form of a serpent, was sharing the couch of his wife.

And so, for one reason or another, there were those who
presented Alexander as believing himself the son of God.
They may have done so either to flatter Alexander or because they thought the story was amusing. Or they may
have hated Alexander, and wished to picture him as a person who had gone completely to pieces. For our own
picture of Alexander we must know the ancient attitude
and understand what some people wanted to believe about

him. This is entirely different from saying that our picture describes Alexander as he was, or that we ourselves can presume to know what was said by Alexander and the priest at the Oasis of Siwah when Alexander himself refused to divulge the conversation.

One purpose of history is to know the possibilities of man, and they are best discovered in those men who developed their own possibilities most fully; obviously, only the precise truth can guide us. Interestingly enough, however, Alexander did propose his own deification years later. This was for a very special reason, as we shall see, and did not imply, in our sense of the word, that Alexander or anyone else thought he was an actual god, although once again we can understand how every kind of fact and story might be brought together to serve a purpose.

Alexander's months in Egypt were profitably spent. The administration of the country was laid down; an Egyptian was appointed governor, but under Alexander's own officers; Alexandria was taking form, at least in outline; a difficult journey had been made across the desert to a famous oracle.

And there was one other thing of far-reaching importance. Plutarch tells us that Alexander met in Egypt a philosopher named Psammon and accepted his teaching that all mankind are under the kingship of God, since in every case that which gets the mastery and rules is divine. Even more philosophical, Plutarch observes, was Alexander's own opinion that although God is indeed a common father of all mankind, still, He makes peculiarly

His own the noblest and best of them. How far Alexander had traveled from the smug dictum of Aristotle that all non-Greeks, and especially those of Asia, were slaves by nature! The conclusion seems inescapable that Alexander was well aware that victory would inevitably bring peace. Peace, however, was bound to have its own special challenge, because contact with "barbarians," on the battlefield and off, was convincing him of the essential sameness of all people. Alexander once summed it up by saying that people should consider as akin to themselves all good men, and as foreigners, only the wicked.

We have already seen that Alexander's confused century was witnessing a growing humanity and universalism. For example, the Athenian orator, Isocrates, gave it a Greek emphasis when he said, "Greeks they are called who share in our culture rather than our descent." Alexander's own belief in the superiority of Hellenism and the possibility of having it the common culture of his empire may have been influenced by Isocrates. And Psammon may have brought him a step farther along by making him realize that a new attitude toward the world might become the driving force of his empire. We may be sure, however, that Alexander's best and most insistent teacher was the non-Greek, a brave fighter, a skillful administrator, and endowed with good and bad qualities in apparently the same proportion as the Greeks themselves.

But Alexander's immediate task, that of completely overwhelming Darius, still remained and was doubtless uppermost in his thoughts.

IX

LORD OF ASIA

ALEXANDER and his men were in high spirits when they left Egypt (spring, 331 B.C.). Their route went up the Phoenician coast and then, with the fertile land, to the Euphrates and across northern Mesopotamia to the Tigris. There was a nearly total eclipse of the moon during the halt on the other side of the river (September 20, 331 B.C.), a phenomenon that has often caused panic in armies. To reassure his men that this was merely a natural occurrence, without religious significance, Alexander sacrificed to the moon, the sun, and the earth; and the seer Aristander reported that the sacrificial victims promised victory that very month. Then scouts rode in to say that Darius and his army were encamped not far off, near the village of Gaugamela, though the town of Arbela (Erbil), thirty-five miles away, popularly gives its name to the battle that soon took place.

Darius had been busy gathering his army ever since he had written Alexander at Tyre, offering a large ransom for his family, marriage to a daughter, all lands west of the Euphrates, and alliance with himself. Alexander had haughtily replied that he already had everything that Darius offered and that if he wished friendship, the Persian must come to him.

Busy as Darius had been, he had really not had sufficient time to reconstitute an army that had been broken at Issus two years earlier. The entire empire had been drawn on for troops, some of them excellent and numerous, but there remained a shortage of good infantry.

To make certain that the mistake of Issus, where he had been hampered by lack of space, would not be repeated, Darius chose for the coming conflict a broad flat plain; some of the ground was leveled for the scythe-bearing chariots which, he hoped, would break the Macedonian phalanx. Persians and Macedonians were always quick to learn about technical matters from one another, and the Persian staff now armed their excellent cavalry with short spears, since their javelins had proved unwieldy in the past. One mistake, however, Darius did make, and that was to keep his men under arms the night before the battle. Consequently, they were not as fresh as their adversaries.

Darius had expected a surprise attack. This course was actually urged on Alexander, but after he had prepared his camp, he told his soldiers to eat and sleep. He himself spent some time in front of his tent with Aristander, celebrating certain mysterious sacred rites and sacrificing to the god Fear. Meanwhile, Parmenio and some of the older officers looked across the plain at all the campfires of the enemy and listened to the tumult of voices rising from their camp as if from a vast ocean; it seemed clear to them that they could not repel such a tide of war in broad daylight. Therefore, as soon as Alexander had finished his sacrifices, they went to him and urged him to attack the enemy immediately, while it was still dark. Alexander realized the confusion and dangers that might develop during a night attack, but once again he gave them the answer they could understand: "I will not steal my victory," he replied. He then went to bed and slept.

He slept so soundly that the officers on their own accord next morning issued orders to the soldiers to take their breakfast. Finally, since the occasion was indeed an urgent one, Parmenio went into Alexander's tent and called him several times by name. When he had roused him, he asked how he could possibly sleep as if he were victorious, instead of being about to fight his greatest battle. Alexander smiled and asked Parmenio if he did not realize that they were already victorious, since they no longer had to march around in search of Darius. He then dressed in his armor and came out of his tent. It was October 1, 331 B.C.

Several special problems confronted Alexander. One of these was the scythe-bearing chariots (far less in number, however, than the two hundred of legend); fifteen elephants with Darius were another problem; but gravest of all was the fact that Darius' troops would extend beyond both Macedonian wings. Accordingly, Alexander drew up his troops in a square. He himself commanded the Companion Cavalry on the right wing of the main line; the phalanx and other infantry were in the center; Parmenio and the superb Thessalian cavalry held the left. In front of the phalanx, as protection against the chariots, were slingers, archers, and javelin-men. The main front line was of necessity shorter than usual, since Alexander was sure that he would be surrounded. Therefore, behind each wing he stationed a column of troops, with orders to attack the Persians on the flank if they came that way. The fourth side of the square was made up of mercenaries, directly behind the phalanx, with orders to wheel around and face the enemy if the Persians attacked from the rear. Altogether, Alexander had about forty thousand infantry and seven thousand cavalry, his largest army thus far.

Darius was in the center of his own line, towering aloft in his chariot and surrounded by infantry, spearmen, Persian and Indian cavalry; in front were archers, scythe-bearing chariots, and the fifteen elephants. The two thousand Greek mercenaries, all that Darius now had, were posted directly opposite the Macedonian phalanx, as high a compliment as could be paid the Greek infantry. The left wing, opposite Alexander, was commanded by Darius' cousin, an extraordinary prince of Bactria named Bessus. His troops included a thousand Bactrian cavalry, a thousand mailed Saca cavalry from far-off Sogdiana in the northeast corner of the empire, and some scythe-bearing chariots. Mazaeus, a Persian, commanded the right wing, opposite Parmenio; with him were Parthians and Medes, scythe-bearing chariots, Armenian and Cappadocian cavalry. Darius' strength and hopes lay in the chariots and the cavalry. The elephants were mismanaged and played no important part in the battle. Altogether, Darius' army was larger than Alexander's, but probably only slightly so—a far cry from the million infantry and forty thousand cavalry of legend.

The Persian order of battle was captured afterward, but we have to supply in our own imagination the speeches Darius made to his men. On his side, Alexander spoke of the need of discipline; he said that it was necessary to keep perfect silence when it was expedient to advance in silence, but at the right moment a great shout and a terrible battle cry were to be raised. He also reminded them that they would not be fighting for Phoenicia or Syria, as hitherto, but for the whole of Asia, to decide who would rule the continent. And in this he was right; the battle of Gaugamela determined for centuries to come whether the overlordship of Hither Asia was to be Asiatic or European, and therefore it must be acclaimed as one of the most decisive conflicts in antiquity.

When all was in readiness, Alexander mounted Bucephalus. Shifting his spear to his left hand, with his right he appealed to the gods to defend and strengthen the Greeks and Macedonians. Aristander, in a white mantle and with a crown of gold on his head, rode along the ranks pointing to an eagle that soared above Alexander's head and then flew straight against the enemy. The sight filled them all with great courage.

The battle opened with Alexander steadily leading his troops to the right. Darius suddenly realized that, if Alexander persisted, the chariots would get into uneven ground, beyond the ground that had been cleared for them. The chariots, therefore, were ordered to charge, but the javelin-men and other light-armed troops in front of the Macedonian line killed some of the horses; the riders of others they dragged to the ground; the chariots that reached the main line found that the Macedonians, following instructions, opened ranks and let them through. At the same time, Bessus sent his cavalry against Alexander's right; there was hard fighting, but in the course of it a gap opened in the Persian line.

Alexander's reaction was instantaneous. He made a wedge of the Companion Cavalry and a part of the phalanx and, raising a loud battle cry, led a rapid charge straight toward Darius. The hand-to-hand fighting was fierce. Alexander told his men to strike the Persians in the face with their spears. (Julius Caesar, a good student of history himself, gave his men exactly the same instructions when he met Pompey at Pharsalus in 48 B.C., explaining that young bachelors would hate to go home with such scars.) The rest of the Macedonian phalanx now pressed forward with its bristling spears until finally Darius, fearing for his life, once again was the first to turn and flee.

Parmenio, however, was having difficulty on the left

wing. While Mazaeus attacked him in flank, some of the Indian and Persian cavalry broke right through the Macedonian line and raced on to rifle Alexander's baggage camp in the rear. Parmenio appealed to Alexander for help. The message reached Alexander just as he was setting off in pursuit of Darius. He promptly returned, but by this time word of Darius' flight had spread, and the various troops of the Persians decided it was sensible to follow suit. Alexander met them just as they had resolved on flight, with the result that the fiercest cavalry engagement in the entire battle now took place. The two groups of cavalry met head on; there was no room for throwing spears or maneuvering. Rather, each man pressed on as best he could. Each fought for his own life, killed wherever possible, and never gave quarter. Sixty of Alexander's Companions fell in this encounter, and several of his friends, including Hephaestion, were wounded.

The Persian rout was now general, and Alexander started in pursuit of Darius once again. He kept up the chase as long as there was daylight, then he rested his cavalry till midnight, and again pursued as far as the town of Arbela, thirty-five miles from the battlefield. Darius, however, made good his escape, for Alexander had been long detained by Parmenio's plight. As he had done after Issus, he captured Darius' chariot, bow, and arrows.

Darius picked up various troops as he fled—Bactrian cavalry, those of the two thousand Greek mercenaries who survived, and others. With them he made straight for Media. Darius had guessed, quite correctly, that Alexander would take the short and easy road to Babylon and Susa, which were real prizes of war. As for Alexander himself, he probably assumed that Darius might give incidental trouble in the future, but it was clear that he could never do more than that. Mazaeus had made good his escape, as had Bessus, the Bactrian prince, and perhaps this was ominous. For the moment, however, it must have seemed to Alexander that no army would ever be able to fight him again; surely, nothing remained except to examine the vast area of the empire he had overthrown, make his might known, and establish order and responsible government.

Alexander returned to Gaugamela from the pursuit to take part in the general rejoicing. He made magnificent sacrifices to the gods and rewarded his friends with gifts of money and property. He was proclaimed King of Asia, and soon began to refer to himself from time to time as Lord of Asia. Then, having founded two cities to protect his communications and police the neighborhood, he set out for the famous and glorious capitals of the ancient Near East.

As Alexander approached Babylon, Mazaeus, Parmenio's gifted opponent at Gaugamela, led the people from the city to offer formal surrender. They were anxious to please and impress the Macedonians in every way, not only by immense presents, but also by the wonders of the place. For example, it was not uncommon in this part of the world for oil to bubble up from the ground, but it was a new phenomenon to the western invaders. One evening, as it was getting dark, the Babylonians took some of the oil and sprinkled it on a street. Then, standing at one end of the street, they put torches to the oil. With the speed of thought, says Plutarch, the flames spread to the other end and the whole street was on fire.

Instead of treating the Babylonians as a conquered people, Alexander did all that he could to reconcile them to his regime, a necessary step if he was to create anything more than another despotism. His administrative arrangements in Egypt had confirmed his attitude toward non-Greeks, an attitude that had already been manifested in Asia Minor. Once again, he appointed a "barbarian" as satrap, none other than the Persian Mazaeus. The military and financial posts at Babylon went to Macedonian officers, however, for apparently Alexander felt that in these matters haste should be made slowly. Religion was something else. In this ancient land it could be turned into a formidable political weapon. Since Xerxes had destroyed the temple of Marduk, Alexander ordered that it should be rebuilt, together with any others that had been damaged by the Persians. He himself sacrificed to Marduk and went through all the religious rites the Chaldaean seers directed.

Susa, the administrative capital of the Persian Empire, was an even richer prize. Through the generations the Great Kings had stored up here no less than 50,000 talents (approximately $90,000,000) in coin and bullion; jars of water from the Nile and Danube, symbolic of the universality of the mighty rulers' sway, and other treasures now fell by right of conquest to Alexander. In celebration, sacrifices were offered, torch races and gymnastic contests were held. All of this was part of a plan to keep the soldiers busy and to introduce the people of the region to the ways of the Greeks. Alexander appointed a Persian as satrap of Susa, and sent another off to Armenia as satrap. He also dispatched money to Antipater, the Macedonian regent, to help him in his forthcoming struggle with Sparta. At the same time, large reinforcements reached Alexander.

Then came a more normal and familiar type of existence for the Grand Army. Persis, the homeland of the Persians, could be reached only through mountainous terrain. Long ago Alexander had discovered the principle, "March divided and fight united." This practice enabled his own column to travel light, while the baggage train could proceed more leisurely under proper escort. He now sent most of the troops and the baggage with Parmenio along the regular road, while he himself and some picked troops headed for the Persian Gates, the rugged mountain pass that served as entrance into Persis.

Here Alexander found that Ariobarzanes, the proud Persian satrap, had built a wall across the pass and stood ready to defend it with forty thousand infantry and seven hundred cavalry, or so, at least, it was reported. A preliminary assault quickly convinced Alexander that this was going to be a very difficult proceeding. Therefore, he left Craterus, an experienced general, in camp before the wall, while he himself with relatively few men made a turning movement. He went quickly over the hills, though it was night, with a prisoner as guide. The Macedonians overwhelmed and killed the Persian sentinels, and just at dawn Alexander assaulted Ariobarzanes' camp in the rear. Bugles signaled Craterus to attack at the same time, so that the enemy was caught from two sides and killed at close quarters. There was a general panic. Those who tried to flee threw themselves over the cliffs and died. Ariobarzanes and a few horsemen escaped.

Alexander raced on to Persepolis, the capital, and arrived before the Persians could do it any harm (February, 330 B.C.). Here and in Pasargadae (the former capital, where Cyrus the Great, founder of the Achaemenid dynasty of the Persians, lay buried) he seized immense treasures, furniture, purple dye, and 126,000 talents in coin and bullion (approximately a quarter of a billion dollars). Alexander not only put this money into circulation, but also started a number of large public works. In this way he distributed much of the Persian wealth among many individuals, in itself not inappropriate. Alexander devoted strict and constant attention to the trade and prosperity of his empire; for example, a standard currency for the civilized world would make easier the exchange of goods, and he ordered his various mints to adopt the well-known Attic standard, the one used at Athens.

These things give us important glimpses into Alexander's manifold activities, but there was another, and not so happy, side to it. His gifts to friends, and even to unknown persons, were so large that his generosity can be described as lavish waste. Olympias once complained to him that he was making his friends the equal of kings. One Macedonian, for instance, wore silver nails in his boots; another had bath powder brought on camels from Egypt; still others used myrrh rather than olive oil in their baths. Finally, Alexander asked the recipients of his bounty if they did not remember that those who conquer by toil sleep better than those who are conquered by their toil. They should see, he added, by comparing their own lives with those of the Persians, that it is a servile thing to be luxurious, but a royal one to toil, for the object of conquest is to avoid doing the same thing as the conquered.

To give his men an example, so we are told, Alexander exerted himself more and more in military and hunting expeditions and even risked his life on many occasions. Once a Spartan envoy met him just as he was bringing down a huge lion and remarked, "You have struggled nobly with the lion, Alexander, to see which should be king."

Alexander's friends, however, became increasingly interested in enjoying their new-found wealth and resented the long marches. At first, Alexander ignored the advice of his critics and said that it was the lot of a king to confer favors and yet be abused. Ultimately, however, so many Greeks, Macedonians, and others betrayed his trust that he lost discretion when he was maligned, and was cruel and inexorable.

Alexander spent some quiet weeks in Persepolis, which at least gave him the opportunity to think. It is tempting to guess that he now busied himself with large plans and extraordinary ideas, for the next couple of years were to see a veritable flood of them. We do know, however, that he appointed a Persian as satrap of Persis and received word that Antipater had overwhelmed the Spartans. "While we were conquering Darius," Alexander observed, "a battle of mice seems to have been fought in Greece."

The weeks must also have been nervously and triumphantly exhausting for Alexander. Here he was, in the heartland of Persia, conqueror of the largest empire the Western world had ever seen, and to it he had added his native Macedonia and Greece as well. We are told that when he first took his seat under the golden canopy on the royal throne of Persia, Demaratus of Corinth, an old friend, burst into tears and declared that those Greeks were deprived of great pleasure who had died before seeing Alexander seated on the throne of Darius.

And there is the famous story of the banquet in the royal palace. A large company had gathered, officers and women, too. Among them was a mere nobody named Thaïs, an Athenian woman, the mistress of Ptolemy. After much drinking she said that it would give her great pleasure, after wandering all over Asia, to set fire to the palace of Xerxes, so that future generations might say that the women with Alexander had inflicted greater punishment on the Persians than all their generals had on Greece. There was tumultuous applause and then, with Alexander leading the way, a garland on his head and shouting joyfully, the whole company took their torches and burned the palace.

It is a fanciful tale, one that posterity had to invent.

Not that Alexander did not set fire to the palace; the excavations of the University of Chicago prove it. More to the point, however, is that both Arrian and Plutarch tell us that Alexander's act was deliberate and premeditated and that he promptly gave orders to put the fire out. It was another of his dramatic acts, designed to reveal to all manner of men a great fact or a fundamental policy. The world now knew, without any question, that the Achaemenid rule of the Persians had come to an end forever and had been succeeded by that of another. What the future held for humanity at large was something Alexander would soon begin to unfold.

X

TRAGEDIES AND DREAMS

I<small>N</small> late March, 330 B.C., word reached Alexander that Darius was at Ecbatana (Hamadan), the ancient capital of the Medes. The Persian had already sent his women and baggage eastward and, in the event that Alexander moved, planned to follow them. He would go, it was said, all the way to Bactria and lay waste the land as he did so. By now, Darius had been reduced to three thousand cavalry and six thousand infantry, but his troops included the surviving Greek mercenaries, the excellent Bactrian cavalry and some remarkable leaders, such as Bessus.

Alexander left Persepolis as soon as he received the message and marched rapidly north, but as he approached Ecbatana, he learned that Darius had fled five days earlier.

Instead of pursuing Darius immediately, Alexander

halted at Ecbatana. Exactly why he did this is not now wholly clear, but we may be sure that there was compelling reason. There is some evidence that he was having trouble with his officer corps; moreover, Ecbatana was probably the farthest point east that men of Alexander's generation were likely to know about. Where, many people must have asked, was Alexander going now? Had not the war ended?

For whatever reason, Alexander decided that, before disappearing into the desert after Darius, it would be wise to make certain things very clear, and this was best done by reconstructing the Grand Army. The burning of the palace at Persepolis had signalized the death of the Persian Empire. During the relatively quiet weeks in the capital, Alexander had apparently evolved still other plans, and now was the obvious time to put the most important and dramatic of them into effect. This plan was the dismissal of his Greek allies. He gave each man his pay and a present, and said he might go home, or if he preferred to stay, he could reenlist as an individual. Many of the Greek soldiers chose to stay with Alexander.

This represents a fundamental turning point in Alexander's career. It meant that the Panhellenic War of Revenge was finished. The League of Corinth could still be a useful instrument in dealing with the Greek cities, but Alexander's special partnership with the Greeks in war was over. Henceforth it was an imperial, not an allied army that marched.

Since he had brought 180,000 talents (approximately

$324,000,000) to Ecbatana (he had also concentrated vast treasures elsewhere), Alexander decided to create the post of Imperial Treasurer. To it he appointed Harpalus, a friend of his boyhood days. As satrap of Media, Alexander appointed a Persian. Then, since he planned to make a sweep to the Caspian Sea as soon as he had finished with Darius, he ordered Parmenio to march by a more direct, though unusual, route and to cut off the people of the region in the rear.

Parmenio, however, disobeyed Alexander's orders and remained in Ecbatana. This was a significant bit of evidence of the general's disloyalty at this time. Perhaps it was inevitable that Macedonian dissatisfaction with Alexander should find its chief expression in Parmenio. He was an older man, Philip's great general, and doubtless he felt that Alexander had already conquered enough. He had said as much at Tyre, when Alexander received Darius' letter offering alliance. Parmenio's disobedience did him little good, for he was soon relieved of his command and ordered to remain in Ecbatana. His execution lay in the not distant future.

Alexander's execution of Parmenio must be judged, partially at least, in the light of a disloyalty that might have endangered Alexander's future military operations.

Now, however, Alexander set off after Darius. Though soldiers and horses fell by the wayside, he went at top speed from Ecbatana to Rhagae, near Teheran, a distance of two hundred miles. On the next day he covered the fifty miles to the Caspian Gates, on the edge of the Parthian desert. Here he learned from deserters that Bessus had arrested Darius. With picked troops and food for two days, Alexander marched all night and till noon the next day; he rested his men briefly and then again marched all night. At dawn he arrived at a village where Darius' army had camped the day before. The natives told him of a shortcut, across a piece of desert wholly destitute of water.

Alexander decided immediately on the shorter route, but he saw that his infantry could not maintain the pace. Since he could not be sure of the quality of the troops with Bessus, he needed the infantry, and so he ordered five hundred horsemen to dismount and told his best heavy-armed infantry to take their place. Alexander then led his men on at a rapid pace. Everyone was thirsty. Some Macedonians found a little water and brought it to Alexander in a helmet, but he gave it back to them. They shouted his praises, and off they went again. They covered fifty miles that night, making a total of two hundred miles in the five days since they had left Rhagae.

Just before dawn, Alexander and the sixty men who had been able to keep up with him burst into the enemy's camp at Hecatompylos (Damghan). The place was in utter confusion; gold and silver lay scattered about, and driverless wagons full of women and children were careening here and there. The leaders had stabbed Darius and fled.

The Macedonians found Darius dying in a wagon, his body torn by javelin thrusts. A soldier gave him some water to drink, and then, with a message of thanks to

Alexander for having treated his family kindly, the former Great King died.

Just then Alexander, who had been pursuing the fugitives, returned. He threw his cloak over Darius' body and ordered that it be taken to Darius' mother at Persepolis for royal burial (early May, 330 B.C.). Alexander had been lucky not to have had the living Darius on his hands, for he was soon to find that nationalism was a very real thing in Iran.

The Caspian Sea, to which Alexander turned before taking up the pursuit of Bessus, fascinated him. Was it by any chance a northern gulf of that Ocean which surrounded the inhabited earth? He proposed to find out, as a student of Aristotle would surely do, and took steps to organize an exploring expedition. His troops, however, had an entirely different idea about all this. They had had enough fighting and wanted to go home. And so, for the first time in his life, Alexander was faced with a real mutiny. Obviously, Parmenio had not been the only one who opposed him. Alexander made a skillful speech that played upon the fears and greed and loyalty of the men, and so brought them back to their duty.

But he did not let it go at that. Since the Greeks had lost their special relation to Alexander and marched as members of the imperial army and not as allies, he now boldly resolved to put another idea into effect. Its general design was to bring both Greeks and Macedonians down from their conception of themselves as the privileged conquerors of Asia, and at the same time to boost the morale of the Asiatics. This is why he decided to wear Persian dress occasionally in public, a dramatic notice to non-Greeks that they, too, counted in the new scheme of things. The Greeks and Macedonians did not like this, and in time the report went round that Alexander had surrendered himself to Oriental luxury and downright degeneracy.

Alexander, however, had realized that the simple gesture of wearing Persian dress might help him gain a great end—the reconciliation of Asia to himself. There were those who later said that he conquered the bodies of the Asiatics with his army, but that he won over their souls with his clothing. Clearly, Alexander was making a deliberate effort to win the minds of his former enemies, even though it cost the pride of the Greeks and Macedonians. As a result, he himself, striving to create a new kind of society for mankind, grew ever more solitary. He once remarked that Hephaestion was the only one of his friends who understood and approved what he was doing.

Meanwhile Bessus, the cousin and murderer of Darius, had headed for his native Bactria and soon began to call himself the Great King. Alexander's plan was to follow him by the direct road east, but an armed uprising on his flank forced him to turn south into Drangiana (Seistan). It was here that he learned of the conspiracy of Philotas, which in turn led to the execution of Parmenio, one of the great tragedies in Alexander's life. Philotas was the son of Parmenio, and Alexander's friend since boyhood. Like so many others of his generation, Philotas was living in a proud and majestic manner; even Parmenio once said to him, "My son, pray be less of a personage."

But when, it was being asked with ever greater insistence, would Alexander stop his fighting and marching and let his friends enjoy their wealth? And why his strange ideas and actions? In the past, the Macedonian kings had associated freely with the nobles, who were practically their equals, but Alexander had become aloof. The opposition of the Macedonian nobility centered rather naturally in Philotas, an officer of considerable prominence. Philotas also had his own personal reason for plotting against Alexander, because of the recent removal of his father from his command.

Ever since the battle of Issus, Alexander had been receiving reports of Philotas' disloyalty, but he had done nothing about it. Now, however, an unimportant Macedonian conspired against Alexander; a couple of youths discovered it and went to Philotas, demanding that they be brought to Alexander at once. Philotas refused their request twice, and so they applied to someone else and were admitted to Alexander's presence. When Alexander showed concern at the whole story, Philotas' enemies had their chance and lodged all kinds of accusations against him. As a consequence, Philotas was arrested.

According to Macedonian law, conspirators against the king were to be tried by the army. Philotas confessed at his trial that he had heard of the plot and yet had said nothing about it to Alexander, even though he visited the royal tent twice a day. The army found Philotas

guilty of treason and, as Macedonian law required, put
him and the other conspirators to death by throwing
javelins at them.

This was not the end of the matter, however. Another
Macedonian law stipulated that relatives of a conspirator
against the king must also die. Therefore, according to
Arrian, Alexander sent orders to the generals in Ecbatana
who had succeeded Parmenio, to put the old man to
death.

How should we judge Alexander's execution of Parmenio? Alexander had followed Macedonian law to the
letter. Parmenio was an old and valued friend of the royal
family, and he had fought well for Alexander. Philotas
had also fought well for Alexander, as had two other of
Parmenio's sons. All were now dead. Should Alexander,
therefore, have overlooked the law? Should he, in the
midst of hard campaigning in Asia, have been loyal to
friends no longer loyal to him? He had decided instantly
that he would remove opposition to himself and his imperial plans by enforcing the law and executing the
famous. This, surely, would bring lesser men to their
senses. Events were to prove him wrong, but Alexander
had shown himself relentless and single-minded long ago
at Tyre, and he was not likely to change now.

Parmenio's treason trial behind him, Alexander resumed his pursuit of Bessus. As he crossed Arachosia
(Afghanistan), he must have been tempted to continue
down the Khyber Pass and so to the fabled land of India.
But reports of serious trouble kept coming to him from

eastern Iran. Bactria (northern Afghanistan) and Sogdiana (Russian Turkestan) were up in arms. Accordingly,
Alexander spent the winter of 330–329 B.C. at the foot
of the Hindu Kush Mountains, waiting for the snows to
melt. There the army was put to work founding a great
satrapal seat near Cabul, the capital of modern Afghanistan. The city was called Alexandria of the Caucasus, for
Alexander believed that the Hindu Kush was an extension
of the Caucasian range in the west.

With the coming of spring, Alexander and the army
began their northward march across the imposing barrier
of the Hindu Kush. The season was still early, and it
was decided to go by the long but relatively low Khawak
Pass (11,600 feet high); even at this lower altitude, the
troops suffered severely from the snow and lack of provisions. Eventually, they crossed the mountains into Bactria, known as the Jewel of Iran and "the land of a
thousand cities," whose capital, Bactra (Balkh), was
called "the paradise of the earth." But they found that
the whole country for miles around had been laid waste
by Bessus and his two powerful allies, Oxyartes and
Spitamenes. As Alexander approached, Bessus and his
allies withdrew across the Oxus River (Amu Daria) into
Sogdiana, and the Bactrians, abandoned by their protec-
tors, surrendered to Alexander. He appointed a Persian as
their satrap.

Alexander could not have known that in eastern Iran
the longest and stiffest resistance in his career faced him.
Two years (329–327 B.C.) of guerrilla warfare, sparked

by Iranian nationalism, lay ahead. Sickness, wounds, treachery, ambush, and murder became the regular order of the day. Nevertheless, Alexander crystallized and gave expression to his extraordinary scheme for mankind.

It came about in a curious way. After he had occupied Bactra, Alexander started for the Oxus River and Bessus. At just this moment, the Thessalian cavalry mutinied. These superb horsemen had been directly under Parmenio's command and had fought with distinction at Gaugamela and throughout the whole expedition. The execution of their great commander rankled, and the prospect of still more fighting at the ends of the earth was too much. Alexander had no alternative but to send them home to Greece.

Alexander's predicament was now acute. Here he was, in distant Asia, without some of his best troops. Although reinforcements were reaching him regularly, he could not summon up replacements at a moment's notice. The success of the entire expedition was at stake, even, perhaps, the lives of them all. Should he, too, return westward?

If Alexander's record shows anything, it is that he never backed away from anything voluntarily. Unless he was to admit failure and go back, there was only one choice left to him now—that was to take a chance and enlist the necessary new troops from the surrounding areas, from the barbarian world itself. And so, for the first time in history, large numbers of Asiatics were added to a European army. Necessity, sheer military necessity, forced this unique experiment on Alexander.

Alexander now entrusted his own life, the lives of his men, and the success of the whole expedition in large part to foreigners—in fact, to foreigners who had just been conquered. Self-interest is one of the most potent forces in history, and in every century, including our own, men have furthered it in various ways. Alexander chose the way of cooperation between races. If the experiment should pay off, if these Asiatic troops should prove loyal and efficient, then the most important step toward the realization of a universal state had already been taken. The immediate future would inevitably produce other, and perhaps more strikingly dramatic refinements, because the world would now be seen in terms larger than Aristotle's narrow concept of an exclusively Hellenic world. There could be nothing more vital and fundamental, however, than the joint effort of different peoples to ensure the success of a common endeavor involving, moreover, physical survival itself.

When Alexander reached the Oxus River with his Asiatic troops, he found that Bessus had burned all the boats. A bridge was out of the question, for there was no timber in the region. Alexander therefore told his men to take the skins used for tent covers, stuff them with chaff, and sew them up. In this way, during the next five days, the troops floated themselves across the river. Messengers now arrived from Spitamenes saying that he had arrested Bessus and was ready to hand him over. At the last moment Spitamenes fled, leaving Bessus behind in a village. There Alexander's troops captured him. They cut off his nose and his ears and sent him to Ecbatana. There, the council of the Medes and Persians ordered that his body should be tied to two bent trees and rent asunder, not because he had murdered Darius, but because he had opposed Alexander, the new Great King.

It became more and more apparent to Alexander that it would be no easy task to catch Spitamenes. The great Sogdian chieftain had some excellent cavalry; he knew the countryside, the desert tracks and oases, and the rivers that eventually lost themselves in the sands. Moreover, Sogdiana was full of men ready to oppose the western invaders. For this reason, after Alexander occupied the capital, Maracanda (Samarkand), Alexander left troops in several forts while he continued his march. The men left behind in the forts were massacred. Alexander retook the forts and mercilessly slaughtered the enemy by the thousands. He himself was wounded in the leg by an arrow and on the head and neck by a stone.

News that Spitamenes was besieging Maracanda reached Alexander at a critical moment. He was at the Jaxartes River (Syr Daria), the northernmost limit of the Persian Empire, and was eager to make his might known in the wholly unfamiliar world beyond. He decided that a detachment of about two thousand men would be enough to defeat Spitamenes, and sent them off under Pharnuches, an interpreter who seemed skillful in dealing with the natives.

Alexander himself set to work founding a city, which he called Alexandria the Farthest (Chodjend). In twenty days the fortification walls of mud bricks were finished, barbarians and unfit soldiers were chosen as settlers, and the usual sacrifices and athletic contests were held. It seemed an ideal bulwark against the nomads across the river.

These nomads were known to the Greeks as "Scythians," a name often applied to people who lived beyond the pale of civilization. They now came down to the edge of the Jaxartes and hurled insults at Alexander and dared him to cross, just as they had formerly challenged the Persian kings. If for no other reason, Alexander decided that he had better teach them a lesson; besides, he had once crossed the Danube and had marched into the Libyan desert on another occasion to secure his frontier, and the same precautions were necessary here.

Once more Alexander gave orders for the tent skins to be stuffed with straw and prepared for crossing and the formal sacrifices to be performed. Aristander, however, announced that the omens were unfavorable, and they remained unfavorable when he took the sacrifices a second time. Aristander had often been useful to Alexander in the past, but now the seer was interpreting religious matters in a way to thwart him. Obviously, he was being used by the Macedonian nobility to further their own interests and, if at all possible, bring Alexander's marches to an end; Callisthenes, the historian, was also involved. Alexander had evidently been quite mistaken, when he thought that the execution of Parmenio would leave him with a free hand.

Just as soon as the skins were prepared for crossing,

Alexander announced that he would disregard omens that promised danger to himself, and ordered his men to get ready for the assault on the Scythians. First, the catapults were placed at the edge of the river and began to send volleys of missiles at the nomads on the opposite bank. Some of the Scythians were wounded, others were killed, and in terror they withdrew a little. Alexander at once ordered the bugles to be sounded, and led the way across the river. Archers and slingers were the first to land, and they started shooting at the Scythians to keep them at a distance until the infantry and cavalry were across. A real, but utterly strange, battle then commenced, for the Scythians used the tactics of the desert, riding round and round the enemy, killing and then dispersing, only to form again. This method of fighting came to be known to the Western world as Parthian tactics; as much as three centuries after Alexander's day Roman legions and their commanders could be overwhelmed by them.

In a flash, Alexander mixed archers and other light troops with the cavalry, broke up the wheeling tactics of the enemy, and then charged. The enemy fled, but after a while Alexander had to call off the pursuit, for he had drunk some bad water and was suffering from a constant diarrhea. His men carried him back to camp, thus fulfilling Aristander's prophecy, some pointedly remarked.

Meanwhile, when Spitamenes learned that the troops under Pharnuches, the interpreter, were approaching, he left Maracanda and withdrew along the Polytimetus River toward the desert. He prepared an ambush and then, using Parthian tactics, swooped on Pharnuches and his men. With no Alexander to guide them, the Greeks and Macedonians formed themselves into a square and in rather disordered fashion tried to get back across the river. Every one of them was killed. When he heard this news, Alexander took some picked troops and, averaging forty-five miles a day for three days, at dawn of the fourth reached Maracanda, which was again under siege by Spitamenes. Spitamenes, however, skipped off to the desert when the Macedonians arrived, and Alexander withdrew to Bactra for the winter.

Pharasmanes, king of the Chorasmians, now came to Alexander and offered to help him conquer the areas stretching westward to the Black Sea. Or, at any rate, that is the way Alexander interpreted his offer. Actually, what Pharasmanes referred to was the Aral Sea. Alexander had heard of this inland sea, since it was not far off, but he took it to be the Sea of Azov, the northern extension of the Black Sea. Pharasmanes was eager to tell Alexander anything that would please him, and together the two men discussed the possibility of a joint expedition. The ignorance of geography that both displayed is beside the point. What matters is that Alexander told Pharasmanes he wished first to subdue India and then, having the whole of Asia, he would return to Greece and, with Pharasmanes' aid, make an expedition to the Black Sea.

This was the first time, as far as we can now tell, that Alexander ever expressed himself on the subject of another expedition. The former Persian Empire, which was practically equivalent to the civilized world in men's thinking, was to be examined throughout its length and breadth; but military expeditions were not to end there. There would be another expedition in the West, and perhaps another. Here, then, in Bactria, Alexander revealed one more of his ambitious plans—nothing less than world conquest.

The following year (328 B.C.) saw much fighting, especially against Spitamenes. Alexander relentlessly hemmed him in with a series of forts, and eventually Spitamenes' men cut off their leader's head and sent it to Alexander. The guerrilla warfare was proving to the hilt the loyalty and effectiveness of the Asiatic troops Alexander had incorporated in his army. It persuaded him to extend the policy of mixed forces, now no longer an experiment, and to order that thirty thousand native youths should be taught the Greek language and trained in the use of Macedonian weapons. Nothing that he ever did was more unpopular with the Greeks and Macedonians than this, and when the youths joined Alexander on his return to Mesopotamia four years later, it was the partial cause of a mutiny.

The terrific heat of Bactria-Sogdiana, the marching and fighting and treachery, the wounds and sickness, all combined to put everybody's nerves on edge. There was need for relaxation, and to the officers this meant a banquet. One was arranged at Maracanda that summer, and Alexander went, as he often tried to do, so that he might not become isolated from his comrades. Though he rarely drank to excess, as the best ancient sources insist, Alexander on this occasion got drunk. So did the others.

Tempers began to flare when a young man sang some verses ridiculing the generals who had been defeated by Spitamenes at the Polytimetus River. Older, and perhaps more sober, guests were annoyed by the bad taste of the singer, but Alexander hilariously told him to go on. Finally Cleitus, Alexander's friend from boyhood, stretched out his hand and reminded Alexander that it was this right hand of his that had saved Alexander's life at the Granicus and that Alexander had now become great and haughty because of Philip's Macedonians. Moreover, Cleitus persisted, it was a poor thing, when surrounded by enemies as they now were, to insult Macedonians who, though slain in battle, were better than those who laughed at them. A tumult followed. Alexander turned to two Greeks beside him and, with a gesture toward the Macedonians, said, "Don't you feel like demigods among wild beasts?" When Cleitus kept on with his taunts, Alexander hit him with an apple and looked around for his sword. A guard had thoughtfully hidden it.

Ptolemy could see real trouble brewing and pushed Cleitus out of the hall. But Cleitus came back through another door, reciting a line from a play by Euripides, "Alas! in Hellas what an evil government!" And when he heard Alexander calling for him, he cried, "Alexander, here I am, Cleitus!" Alexander then seized a spear from a guard and killed his boyhood friend.

Alexander had committed murder during a drunken

brawl. It was more than a crime, for it was also a great personal tragedy. For three days, Alexander lay in his room, refusing all food and appealing to the names of Cleitus and his sister Lanice, who had been his own nurse. But the Greeks and Macedonians were in a far-off land, surrounded by enemies, and the most important thing at the moment was to restore Alexander to normal health. For this reason the seers said that the avenging wrath of Dionysus, the god of wine, had killed Cleitus, because Alexander had omitted a sacrifice to the god whose birthplace, Thebes, he had destroyed. The historian Callisthenes came and tried to comfort Alexander, but the Sophist Anaxarchus apparently did him the most good. As soon as he entered Alexander's room, he shouted, "Here is Alexander, to whom the whole world is now looking, but he lies on the floor weeping like a slave. Don't you know that Zeus has Justice and Law seated beside him, in order that everything that is done by the master of the world may be lawful and just?"

Sophists and flatterers, artists and philosophers had been coming out to Alexander in increasing numbers with the regular reinforcements. Most of them disliked Callisthenes for his dignified and independent way of life and said that he walked around as if he were the only freeman among so many tens of thousands. The Macedonians in particular hated the historian because, as a Greek, he had once remarked that it was faction among the Greeks that had made possible Philip's victory at Chaeronea, after which remark he had quoted the line, "In a time of sedition, the base man too is in honor."

Callisthenes' remarks irritated Alexander, but the historian refused to hold his tongue. Occasionally he would say to Alexander, quoting Achilles' speech to Hector, "Dead is also Patroclus, a man far braver than you."

Despite the jealousies and quarrels, even despite the plots and mutinies, the expedition operated smoothly enough as a rule. When there was a clash, Alexander won (or, more exactly, he was never deposed), and this was due as much to his heavy hand as to his genius. Years later Cassander, who was one of the half dozen powerful generals in Alexander's entourage to become a king, was walking around Delphi, admiring its many beauties. Suddenly, we are told, he rounded a corner and came on a statue of Alexander, and the mere sight of it made him shudder and tremble.

Alexander and his men took quarters very briefly that winter of 328 B.C., for a certain opponent was causing Alexander special concern. This was the Bactrian Oxyartes, one of Spitamenes' chief allies. Oxyartes had placed his family for safekeeping on a high and precipitous rock; provisions had been stored away against a possible siege; and at the moment (early spring, 327 B.C.), there was deep snow all around. The barbarians yelled insults at Alexander and said he could not take their stronghold unless his soldiers had wings. That night, about three hundred men responded to the taunts of the barbarians. They fixed iron tent pegs in the earth and snow, and then hauled themselves up with ropes. Thirty perished in this fashion, but by dawn the rest had reached the peak behind the fortress and signaled to Alexander. He pointed out his soldiers with wings to the barbarians, and in terror they promptly surrendered.

Oxyartes' daughter, Roxane, was among the captives. The soldiers maintained that she was the most beautiful woman they had ever seen in Asia, with the sole exception of Darius' wife. Roxane and Alexander fell in love with each other at sight, so the storytellers relate, and of course it had to be that way. The young and handsome invader from the West, the beautiful young daughter of an intrepid baron—what else could it be but love? Well, it was doubtless a very sensible way to bring the long guerrilla warfare to an end. Eastern Iran had fought well; now a political marriage might enlist the support of powerful leaders.

Plutarch summed it up when he said that the marriage was "thought to harmonize well with the matters which Alexander had in hand." One of these "matters" was a new and strange idea Alexander had been evolving, the mixture of races; other men were urged to follow his example in marrying a barbarian.

That same spring at Bactra there was another and most extraordinary banquet. With Alexander's approval, the subject of prostration (throwing oneself down in reverence to a deity) was discussed, and with it the advisability of paying homage to Alexander as a divine person. Anaxarchus, the Sophist, opened the subject by saying that since Alexander would surely be honored as a god after his death, it would be ever so much more appropriate and generous to deify him while he lived. Then he and the others at the banquet, chiefly illustrious Persians and Medes, who had concocted the scheme with Alexander, wanted to begin the ceremony of prostration at once.

In spite of a widely held belief today, prostration had no implications of divinity among the ancient Persians; it was merely a mark of respect. But the Greeks reserved prostration for the gods. And so, when Anaxarchus had finished his speech, most of the Macedonians were very angry with him, though they kept silent. Callisthenes, however, delivered a long and vigorous speech in opposition, reflecting, it is said, the exact sentiments of the Macedonians. He greatly displeased Alexander, but Alexander was nevertheless so impressed by the historian's arguments that he gave orders for the idea of deification to be dropped. It was never again brought up by him.

The proposal to deify Alexander was not quite as amazing as would first appear. For one thing, this was an irreligious century, and no one, least of all Alexander, would regard him as an actual god. When the subject was eventually discussed in Athens, the reaction of Demosthenes was typical: "Let Alexander be the son of Zeus, and of Poseidon too, if he likes." Moreover, and very much to the point, the Greeks had often raised prominent men to the ranks of the gods in Alexander's century, not only after their death, but even during their lifetime.

Nevertheless, it was an extraordinary proposal, and we must try to see what was in Alexander's mind. His motivation, we may be sure, must have been a compelling one,

and the only one that will fit him at this particular moment in his life was sheer military necessity. When his
Thessalian cavalry mutinied, drastic action was required.
The same drastic action was required now, for Alexander
was faced with continuing opposition and conspiracies.
We have only to think of Philotas, Parmenio, and Cleitus;
the mutiny of the Thessalians; the resistance of Aristander
and Callisthenes to the crossing of the Jaxartes; the opposition of the Macedonian nobility at the Bactra banquet.
The business of being on good terms with one's generals
and immediate circle was militarily as necessary as the re-
placement of the Thessalians.

Mutinous cavalry could be replaced with cavalry from
the neighborhood, but what was Alexander to do with an
uncertain officer corps? It seems clear that he decided to
abandon the comradely relationship with his officers and
to put an end to lukewarm support and possible plots by
becoming a god, exactly as the ancient writers say. The
explanation, then, is a simple one, and it becomes exceptionally so when we translate it into our own terms.
Alexander had decided that the times required that he
should become officially an autocrat.

Not much later, the royal pages plotted to kill Alexander; the pages were the young sons of Macedonian nobles,
and guarded the king while he slept. The plot was discovered, and when the pages were arrested, they said that
Callisthenes had instigated them. Callisthenes and the
youthful confederates were all put to death.

Aristotle never forgave Alexander for the execution of

his nephew. So great were the philosopher's prestige and influence that literary people quickly adopted a hostile attitude toward Alexander. They set to work creating the familiar picture of the young man who began well enough, but ended as a bloody and lucky despot, the son of God. It is partly this that has made it so difficult to reconstruct the Alexander of history.

Difficult it may be, but far from impossible, when we ourselves distinguish the sound contemporary sources. As an example, let us take Alexander as he kills and dreams in Bactria-Sogdiana. The picture that emerges from a backward glance will be of neither a devil nor a god, but of a man with great faults and virtues, limitations and contradictions, who was well on his way to creating a new society.

Although the expedition itself may have been Alexander's greatest crime, he had never hesitated to invade Asia, for his century was one of conquest—as what century has not been? He inherited from his father the general plan and had no doubt of his own ability to see it through. Almost everywhere he went, he killed, but the Egyptians were not the only ones to welcome him as a deliverer from the misrule of the Persians.

By the time he reached Bactria-Sogdiana, however, Alexander had made it abundantly clear that those who wished to live in peace with him would have peace (on his terms) and prosperity as well. He had started great public works and instituted a uniform currency. He had founded a number of cities, and enlarged others to serve as police instruments. From their Hellenic colonists would spread a common Greek culture, but the barbarian world was also to enjoy responsibility and dignity. He had appointed many barbarians to important administrative posts; thousands were in the army, and other thousands were being prepared for military service. Most of these were Persians, but there were others as well. The Persian dress that Alexander occasionally wore emphasized to the barbarians that he was not only King of Macedonia but their king, too, the Great King of the former Persian Empire. He was also, of course, hegemon of the Corinthian League, the ally of the Greek cities along the coast of Asia Minor, the adopted son of the barbarian queen Ada, and a god in Egypt; soon he was to become the suzerain, or overlord, of Indian rajahs.

Alexander had expressed himself on the subject of world conquest and, of chief importance perhaps, on the fusion of races. He did not have in mind a deliberate Hellenization of the East or a barbarization of the Greeks and Macedonians. The overwhelming majority of people would prefer to pursue their own national life, and they were entirely free to do so; but there was also to develop a new life based on an interchange and mixture of customs and blood. Here, in very truth, was a new attitude toward the world; with success, it would become the driving force, and the cement, of his world empire.

Alexander once said that it was his kingly business to mix all men as in a loving cup. It is little wonder that his union of great ideas with great acts should produce a new world and, more importantly, a new conception of the world, the world of common interests. Looking back on it four centuries later, Plutarch exclaimed passionately: "O Xerxes, stupid fool to spend so much fruitless toil on bridging the Hellespont! This is the way that wise kings join Asia with Europe; not by beams and rafts, but by ties of lawful love and mutual joy in children."

The picture of Alexander by the time he reached Bactria-Sogdiana is one of relentless, brilliant, and often cruel conquest, followed by a real and most unusual peace. But it is necessary to add, and with very considerable emphasis, that it was all to be subject to Alexander's will: he never gave any indication that he planned to abdicate. Even though he failed in his attempt to become officially a god, he remained an autocrat. Ideas and dreams, however, have a way of growing and developing, and in the year before his death Alexander was to show how much he had grown in the interim, for the better and for the worse as well. The very next years were bound to influence him, especially as wondrous India lay just ahead.

XI

INDIA

ALEXANDER and his men knew almost nothing about India. To them it was a land of wonders and riches, at the very ends of the earth, full of innocent, happy people, curious ascetics, and monstrosities. A book of the previous century, written by a Greek physician at the court of the Persian king, told how the author had once seen an Indian monster as big as a lion, with a human face and a tail that shot out stings. This kind of story, and not the narratives of Herodotus and other historians, formed the popular Western concept of India.

Aside from this, Alexander conceived of India as the valley of the Indus River, beyond which was the Punjab, or Land of the Five Rivers; and at that point, or not much farther east, was Ocean, the eastern extremity of the world. One goal for Alexander's universal state was now within his grasp, and so, too, was another, the southern limit of the world, for he had been told that the Indus flowed into Ocean at the south.

Alexander brought sailors and shipwrights with him from the eastern Mediterranean, so that he could build a fleet beside the Indus. After exploring the river's course to its mouth, the plan was to sail across Ocean and establish a regular connection with Egypt, always provided that a sea route actually existed. The eastern and western halves of his empire could then be tied together by trade, and prosperity would be further increased by the cities and harbors that he would build on his eastern and southern frontiers. It was an immense idea.

Alexander also knew that he would have friends as well as enemies in India. Taxiles, the rajah of Taxila (Takshaçila), an ancient city just east of the Indus, had sent envoys to Alexander while he was still in Bactria. The envoys had offered to surrender the city to the Macedonians, for Taxiles was in need of help against his dread enemy, Porus, the ruler of a mighty kingdom beyond the Hydaspes River.

And there were two other things that Alexander knew, or thought he knew. One was that Dionysus and Heracles had reportedly come this way. This was a feat that his adventurous spirit could not overlook. The other thing he knew was decisive. It was simply that the Persian Empire had once stretched into India. The Persian Empire was now his own, and he must see every corner of it.

Then he would press on to the limits of the inhabited earth.

Bactria-Sogdiana had been won at such cost that Alexander left behind 10,000 infantry and 3,500 cavalry to ensure its loyalty. This so depleted his army, despite reinforcements that had reached him, that he set off for India with approximately the same number of soldiers (35,000) as he had had when he crossed the Hellespont. Central Asiatic horse-archers, mounted javelin-men and other barbarian contingents suggested, as nothing else could, the universality of the army and, to Alexander, if not to many others, the universality of the new state that was taking form.

In addition to the soldiers, other thousands marched with Alexander: traders and camp followers, women and children, writers and scientists. Further reinforcements from Greece and the addition of Indian and other barbarian units steadily swelled the total, and Plutarch may be entirely correct when he says that 135,000 people ultimately came back across the Punjab with Alexander.

The Greeks and Macedonians were overjoyed to leave eastern Iran, where they had marched and fought for two terrible years. In the early summer of 327 B.C. they recrossed the Hindu Kush Mountains by the Kaoshan Pass (14,300 feet high). They traveled light, at least for awhile, because Alexander had noticed that the army had accumulated so much booty that it was hardly able to move out of Bactria. He had ordered everything of that kind to be burned. The soldiers had obeyed promptly, for nowadays disobedience meant inexorable punishment.

Punishment, but on a larger scale, was to be Alexander's policy for the years just ahead. The choice that Alexander placed before the teeming population of India, as he moved from one district to another, was immediate surrender or annihilation. The experience of Bactria-Sogdiana, where the guerrilla war had tied him down, was to be avoided at all costs. Slaughter, senseless slaughter, became the new order of the day, unless sheer terror produced submission in advance.

It does not make a very pretty picture. The Indians already had their own way of life and government, and Alexander could hardly justify continuing massacre on the ground that his brand of peace would follow. Hither Asia was one thing: history was to prove that permanent conquest was possible there. But India was too far from Alexander's homeland, and he should have known that he had too few Greeks and Macedonians to realize in India the new society he had in mind. Of all his conquests, India alone reverted to its original condition immediately after his death. In fact, it hardly paid him allegiance in the last year of his life. If he had lived, he might have had the genius to hold and mold so large an empire, but on the evidence, this seems doubtful.

Whatever the future might have held for Alexander, we can be certain of only one thing—that, having crossed the Hindu Kush, he immediately put into effect the plan of ruthless annihilation he had apparently decided upon as a settled policy. He sent Hephaestion and the baggage train, together with various contingents of troops and the Indian princes who had begun flocking to him, down the Cophen River (the Khyber Pass) to the Indus. This route across the Northwest Frontier had always been the historic entrance by land into India. Alexander himself turned to the mountains on his northern flank and commenced the indiscriminate slaughter of entire tribes. Word of his ruthlessness soon spread. On the mere rumor of his approach, the barbarians would fire their cities and flee. But even as he marched and conquered, imperial problems of the most diverse kind were on Alexander's mind. For example, at one town he captured thousands of magnificent cattle and sent the largest and finest of them back to Macedonia to improve the stock there.

The capture of Aornos was Alexander's outstanding military exploit in this part of India. For generations, geographers and travelers have looked in vain for the site of Aornos, and it was only in 1926 that Sir Aurel Stein, the indefatigable and distinguished explorer of innermost Asia, identified it with a ridge now known as Pir-sar. Its location is as breathtaking as the ancient descriptions suggest.

We must think of Pir-sar as consisting of two ridges: the main one, Pir-sar itself, is 7,100 feet high, with cliffs dropping 5,000 feet down into the Indus; Una-sar, the other ridge, is 8,720 feet high and also has cliffs of sheer walls of rock. These two ridges meet at right angles; at the point of meeting, there is a rocky cone, 800 feet high, called Bar-sar. Bar-sar is at the very end of Pir-sar, but is separated from Una-sar by a ravine with precipitous sides, 800 feet deep and 1,500 feet wide. It can all be visualized as an inverted capital L: Pir-sar and its cone of Bar-sar meeting Una-sar at right angles, but separated from it by a ravine. Sweeping in a wide bend, the Indus almost encircles the place.

This, then, is the famous "rock" Aornos which, as its Greek name implies, not even birds could reach. Legend had it that Heracles (Krishna) had once failed in an attempt to assail it. The challenge of the romantic past and the fact that most of the Indians of the neighborhood had fled to the rock for refuge, made Alexander decide to attack it immediately. The ascent and defense of Pir-sar proved too difficult, however, so Alexander concentrated on the other ridge. But it was not until he had actually captured Una-sar that he learned of the deep ravine. He trained his catapults on Bar-sar, the cone opposite, where the enemy were massed, but the distance was too great for the effective use of the engines. There was nothing to do but fill up the ravine with a mound. It took his men four days to extend the mound to a small hillock just below Bar-sar.

Alexander's catapults now began to kill an enemy already thoroughly terrified by the audacious skill of the Macedonian engineers; and when Alexander and seven hundred men scaled Bar-sar, the Indians broke. Most of them were killed in their flight, while others perished by jumping down the precipices.

Meanwhile, Hephaestion had been ordered to bridge the Indus, and when Alexander joined him, he found that all the preparations had been completed. Taxiles, the rajah, had sent rich presents: two hundred talents of silver, seven hundred horsemen, three thousand oxen, ten thousand sheep, and thirty elephants.

If the western invaders still entertained any doubt about the wealth of India, they quickly changed their minds on entering Taxiles' capital, Taxila (spring, 326 B.C.). Taxila was a large and busy city, with interesting bazaars, splendid palaces, and a university conducted by Brahmans. The Greeks looked on the Indians with a certain arrogance, and yet they could not restrain their innate curiosity; perhaps they were really uncomfortable in the presence of India's more ancient civilization. When Alexander came across some Hindu ascetics, or priests, walking in a meadow, for example, they suddenly began to stamp on the ground, saying, "Each man possesses as much of the earth as we have stepped on, Alexander; but you have traveled over a large part of the earth, having trouble yourself and giving it to others. And yet you will soon die and possess only enough of the earth to be buried in."

One of the Brahmans, Calanus, joined Alexander's expedition, to the disgust of his colleagues. It was he who explained to Alexander how to govern. He threw a shriveled hide on the ground; as he walked around its edge, the hide rose up everywhere, but when he stood in the center, it stayed firm and still. The moral was that Alexander should remain in the middle of his empire and not stray far from it.

Some of the Brahmans even refused Alexander's invitation to visit him, insisting that if he was the son of Zeus, they were too. An utterly new world had been suddenly thrust upon the Greeks and Macedonians. How mystified they must have been, on days so hot that it seemed to them hardly possible to walk on the ground with bare feet, to find people actually standing or sitting or lying naked and motionless all day, sometimes on stones or nails! How was this India to be fitted into the new scheme of things?

It was to the advantage of both Alexander and Taxiles to reach a common understanding as quickly as possible. Taxiles hoped for the destruction of his enemy Porus, whose kingdom lay a hundred miles to the east, beyond the Hydaspes River. The new wind from the West might overwhelm Porus and, in the process, blow itself out as well. As for Alexander, he knew that he must get to the river before tropical rains and the melting snows of the Himalayas turned it into a raging torrent. He and Taxiles exchanged gifts and other formalities. Alexander added five thousand Indians to his army and ordered that the warships, already prepared for the voyage down the Indus, be brought in sections to the Hydaspes. He enlarged the kingdom of Taxiles to compensate him for his reduction to the status of a vassal prince under a Macedonian satrap and garrison. And then he set out for the Hydaspes (Jhelum).

It was early June when Alexander arrived. The rains had commenced, and the river was already rising. On the opposite bank, half a mile away, he could see Porus, a magnificent figure of a man, well over six feet tall and mounted on an elephant of appropriate size. Altogether, Porus had more than two hundred elephants, several hundred scythe-bearing chariots, and far more infantry than Alexander. Alexander's superiority lay in his cavalry, but unlike those of Porus, his horses were not trained to the smell and trumpeting of the elephants. How was he to solve this problem? But first, how was he to get across the river? Porus seemed to be constantly on the alert.

Alexander then hit on this stratagem: he ordered his ships to sail up and down the river, and at the same time he divided his army and sent some contingents in one direction, others in another; still other men were told to bring skins to the river's edge and start filling them with hay, as if they were about to cross. The whole western bank of the river was alive with activity and shouting, day after day. And each day Porus marched up and down the river, following Alexander's troops as best he could, but it all came to nothing. Obviously, the Macedonian crossing was purely imaginary, hopelessly impossible. Porus finally tired of it all and, posting scouts along the bank, withdrew to his camp.

Alexander immediately went into action. Eighteen miles above his camp at Haranpur, he had discovered a wooded promontory at Jalapur, where the Indus makes a great bend. An island at just this point would screen any attempt to cross. Alexander secretly sent his ships there and ordered Craterus to prepare openly and noisily a crossing from the main camp at Haranpur. Craterus, who had taken Parmenio's place as the second in command, was given several thousand troops, including the five thousand Indians. Alexander took fifteen thousand picked infantry and cavalry and, keeping far from the river, marched secretly up to Jalapur.

There was a terrible storm that night, but at least the claps of thunder drowned out the noise as the Macedonians prepared to cross. By dawn the weather was better. Alexander entered a ship with some friends—Ptolemy, the future king of Egypt, Perdiccas, who became regent of the empire on Alexander's death, Lysimachus, the future king of Thrace, and Seleucus, who was to inherit the Asiatic part of Alexander's empire. Like the troops, they crossed to the island in boats or on skins. Porus' sentinels did not spot them until they began to cross from the island to the opposite bank. But here Alexander made a mistake. Through ignorance of the topography, he landed his troops not on the farther bank, but on another island. Ordinarily, the island was separated from the shore by a shallow stream, but the rains had turned the stream into a torrent. Fortunately for Alexander, the ford was found, and he and his men were able to cross. The water reached to the shoulders of the infantry and to the heads of the horses.

Almost at once they ran into two thousand troops that Porus had dispatched under his son; the son was killed, and the troops decisively beaten. This put Porus in a quandary, for Alexander was now on his side of the river, and Craterus could be seen preparing to cross from the main camp. Porus decided to leave a few elephants to frighten Craterus' horses, and with the rest of his troops he marched to meet Alexander.

For the encounter, Porus chose a place that was sandy; most of the ground elsewhere was clay and too slippery for bowmen and cavalry. Porus then posted his 200 elephants over a stretch of four miles. At least 100 feet separated each elephant from the next, and in the space between them, but to the rear, Porus placed the infantry. They extended beyond the elephants to the left and right and far outnumbered the troops Alexander had been able to transport across the river. Infantry and elephants, then, formed Porus' center. On each wing were 2,000 cavalry (probably less than Alexander's), with 150 scythe-bearing chariots in front of each wing.

It made an extraordinary sight—at any rate for a European—and when Alexander caught up with the enemy, he told his men to rest while he studied the situation. He had no elephants, and his horses, he knew, would not face the elephants with Porus. The best scheme, he decided, was to strike another part of Porus' army and roll it back on the elephants. Accordingly, he posted the phalanx in the center and told it not to join the action until the enemy's cavalry had been routed by his own attack. He then placed all his cavalry under himself on the right wing.

When Porus saw how Alexander had disposed his army, he made the fatal mistake of transferring all his cavalry to his left wing, opposite Alexander. Alexander's reaction was instantaneous. He sent his Asiatic horse-archers forward to pour a rain of arrows on that part of the enemy's infantry which extended beyond the left flank of the elephants. At the same time, he told Coenus, a very able Macedonian aristocrat, to take half the cavalry, sweep back of the army and around his own left wing and so to the enemy's right, which was now devoid of cavalry. He was then to dash behind Porus' troops and attack their cavalry in the rear.

Porus now had to make his cavalry face both ways, but in the confusion of the change, both Coenus and Alexander charged. Alexander's attack was so sharp that the enemy's cavalry were driven back on the elephants. The drivers of the elephants ordered their beasts forward, but it was too late, for this was the moment when the Macedonian phalanx had been told to charge. The Macedonians kept a wide open formation and hurled their weapons at riders and beasts, until finally the wounded elephants, crazed with pain, rushed madly at friends and foes alike and then, as an ancient writer puts it, "began to retire slowly, facing the enemy like ships backing water, and merely uttering a shrill, piping sound."

Alexander now ordered his infantry to link their shields together and attack, while he and his cavalry surrounded the whole line of the enemy and hemmed them in. Meanwhile, Craterus had crossed the river with his cavalry and was able to pursue fugitives with his fresh troops. The Indians were slaughtered mercilessly.

The battle of the Hydaspes had raged eight hours, and

a general massacre was prevented only by Porus' decision to surrender. He had been wounded in the right shoulder, but nonetheless he stopped his elephant, dismounted, and advanced on foot, full of dignity and apparently unawed by Alexander. Alexander admired his handsome figure and asked him how he wished to be treated. "Like a king," Porus answered, and when Alexander asked him if he had anything else to say, he replied that everything was included in that.

After the battle, the Macedonians made sacrifices to the gods, buried the dead, and staged athletic contests. Alexander then founded two cities, Nicaea (Victory) at Jalapur and, on the battlefield, Bucephala, in memory of his horse, which had died there.

The battle of the Hydaspes—Alexander's fourth and last pitched battle—was especially significant in two respects. In the first place, it had been so desperately fought that the mere mention of elephants had a way of unnerving his men. And secondly, the size and vitality of India had impressed itself on Alexander. He therefore relieved Taxiles of his dependence on the Macedonian satrap and raised him to the status of an independent king. This was to be Porus' position as well. The two Indian rajahs were reconciled to each other, and then, hoping that this loose confederation under himself as suzerain would work, Alexander continued his eastward march across the rivers and plains of the Punjab.

The immensity of India and its population, the intense heat, the monsoon rains, the constant marching and fighting in a completely strange world proved to be more than his men would endure. They knew they had had enough when they stood near Gurdaspur and gazed across the Hyphasis River (Beas) at plains stretching interminably to the horizon, and listened to tales of countless more elephants and even braver Indians awaiting them. They simply refused to go farther. It was one of the most curious mutinies in history, for no one thought of deposing Alexander; he was the only person in the world who could lead them safely home, and home they proposed to go.

Alexander, on the other hand, was determined to march those last few miles to Ocean where, on the eastern extremity of his empire, he planned to found cities, dredge harbors, and build dockyards. He called his officers together and in a passionate speech reminded them of the prosperous world state they were creating. Silence greeted his remarks. Finally Coenus, who had fought so well at the Hydaspes, summoned up his courage and told Alexander that only a few were left of those who had originally marched out of Macedonia with him; those few, he said, were now exhausted and wanted nothing so much as to go home and see their families again. There was prolonged applause when Coenus finished, and some men even shed tears.

Like his ancestor Achilles, Alexander angrily retired to his tent for three days, hoping that the army would change its mind. When it did not, he ordered the sacrifices for crossing the river to be made. It was a surprise to no one that the seers declared the omens unfavorable, and then

Alexander announced the good news, that he would go back.

Memorials of his great march had to be set up, however. Immense altars to the twelve Olympian gods were erected; armor, mangers, and bits for horses, all much bigger than customary, were scattered up and down as reminders of the manner of men who had once come this way. In his heart of hearts, apparently, Alexander knew that he would not be seeing the Punjab very soon again.

XII

THE TERRIBLE RETURN

ALEXANDER'S plans to continue his march across India had been thwarted. But if his ambition to see the eastern extremity of the inhabited earth could not be realized, much else remained. For example, he had left at the Hydaspes the fleet that he had originally planned to use in his sail down the Indus. He had given his men orders to build more ships, for in time he would return and explore the Indus river system as far as Ocean on the south. The moment for the voyage had arrived sooner than he expected, but at any rate he would now put his plan into effect.

Details would have to wait on the future, but certainly further marching and exploration would yield, in large outline, the limits of his empire. In other words, though his men had won their point about not continuing farther east, Alexander chose the route homeward. Not only was it not the direct way back, but it proved to hold continuous fierce fighting, suffering, and near-disaster.

All was hustle and bustle on Alexander's return to the Hydaspes. The new cities, Nicaea and Bucephala, were rising; the Phoenician and other crews from the eastern Mediterranean were ready; and a fleet of between eight hundred and one thousand ships was at hand. Nearchus of Crete, who later wrote a history of his expedition, was appointed admiral of the fleet; another Greek, Onesicritus, was to be the pilot of Alexander's ship. The general plan, as Alexander worked it out, was to sweep everything before him, so that he could reach Ocean as rapidly as possible. Cavalry, infantry, archers and other light-armed troops were to sail with him. Craterus was to march along the right bank, Hephaestion along the left, each with large bodies of men. Inevitably many hostile Indians would slip through the net prepared for them, and so Alexander's cousin, Philip, who had general satrapal oversight of India, was to follow and destroy the fugitives after an interval of three days.

Embarkation began at dawn of a November day in 326 B.C. Alexander sacrificed to the customary gods and also, as instructed by the seers, to the River Hydaspes. From the prow of his ship he poured libations to the Indus and the other rivers that flowed into it, to Heracles and Ammon, and then ordered the bugle to signal the departure. The baggage vessels, the horse transports, and the warships had all received their instructions to keep in line, with a safe distance between boats. Rarely in antiquity did such an immense armada sail together, and it had been created within a matter of months in a distant land. The noise of the rowers and the cries of the boatswains alerted the entire countryside. Indians, full of excitement, swelled the crowd that had assembled to watch the start. Singing their strange songs, they danced along the river's banks until the fleet disappeared from sight.

Most of the Indians in Alexander's line of march opposed him, to their sorrow. He wiped out towns with populations of 50,000 people; he exterminated whole tribes. The Macedonians were not allowing anything to stop their homeward journey. Fugitives were pursued through jungles and across deserts. Gradually the troops tired of it all and would have pressed on regardless of enemies left behind.

At the fortified town of the Malli, who were reputedly the bravest of all the Indians, Alexander ordered the scaling-ladders to be placed against the walls; but when his soldiers were slow to mount, he angrily snatched a ladder and went up himself, followed by three men. The Macedonians became alarmed at the sight of Alexander practically alone on the walls and made a dash for the ladders, which broke under their combined weight. When Alexander saw what had happened, he nevertheless jumped down into the city. His three friends followed him. One was killed at once, the other two were wounded, but were able to fight on with Alexander. An arrow went through Alexander's breastplate and fastened itself in a rib. He sank to his knees, his back propped against the wall, breathing out blood from his wound. Other blows fell on him, and he was near to fainting when the Macedonians, at last fully aroused for his safety, broke into the city and slew every man, woman, and child.

The removal of the arrow proved a difficult operation, and Alexander's convalescence was correspondingly slow. Finally, a report spread that he had died. The soldiers were overwhelmed with fear for their own survival—who now could lead them home through all these enemies, across huge rivers and unknown deserts? They would not believe it when Alexander wrote them that he was alive and would soon join them in their camp. Even when he sailed back to them they would not believe it. They thought the ship bore Alexander's corpse. And so Alexander stretched out his hand to them, and while they cheered, he landed, mounted his horse, and rode to his tent. Those who could, came forward and touched him, others threw garlands on him, and all sang his praises. But Nearchus says that Alexander's close friends reproached him for exposing himself in battle as if he were a private soldier.

In time, Alexander resumed the descent of the rivers. On the way he founded cities at strategic points. Seemingly he had every intention of holding what he had conquered. News of his military skill and his terrible treatment of enemies spread with the result that more and more Indians fled or surrendered on his approach. But the Brahmans were implacable—and a complete mystery as well—to the Greeks and Macedonians.

The story is told, for example, that Alexander captured

ten Indian philosophers, known as Gymnosophists, who were supposed to be very clever at answering questions. He decided to prove their cleverness by asking them difficult questions, and said that those who answered incorrectly would be put to death. He made the oldest Gymnosophist judge.

The first one, being asked by Alexander which were more numerous, the dead or the living, said the living were, since the dead did not exist. The second was asked whether the earth or the sea produced larger beasts; he replied that the earth did, for the sea is but a part of it. The third was asked which animal was the most cunning, and he replied, "That which man has not yet discovered." The fourth was asked why he had persuaded a local ruler to revolt. "Because," he answered, "I wanted him either to live or die nobly." The fifth, being asked which was older, day or night, said "Day, by one day." When Alexander expressed his astonishment, the Indian explained that hard questions had to have hard answers.

Then Alexander asked the next philosopher what a man had to do to be really loved. "He must be very powerful," the Indian replied, "without being feared." The seventh, being asked how a man might become a god, answered, "By doing that which a man cannot do." Alexander asked the next Indian which was stronger, life or death, and he replied, "Life, because it supports so many miseries." And the last, when he was asked how long it was right for a man to live, said, "Until death appears more desirable than life."

Alexander then turned to the judge and ordered him to

give his sentence. The Indian said that in his opinion each had answered worse than another. Alexander finally dismissed them with gifts, as mystified as ever.

The point at which the Hydaspes and the other rivers of the Punjab joined the Indus struck Alexander as ideal for yet another Alexandria. He had the city laid out, complete with harbor and dockyards, and designated it as the southern administrative limit of the Punjab. He left his cousin, Philip, as regent, but the Punjab was practically independent. Alexander's ambitious schemes were in fact little more than a promise to return at a later date, for he had neither the time nor sufficient helpers to do more at the moment. Besides, reports kept coming to him concerning the difficulties of the projected homeward march, and he decided that the sick, the baggage, and the elephants should be sent by a better-known and easier route. He ordered Craterus to take them by way of the Mulla Pass and Candahar to Carmania.

The descent of the rivers was long and arduous, but in July, 325 B.C., Alexander reached the Indus Delta and looked out on Ocean. It must have been one of the most satisfying and thrilling moments in his life. He had been right; there was indeed a southern limit to the inhabited earth, and this was it. He sailed out into the Indian Ocean, to make sure that no more land existed, sacrificed to the customary gods, and prayed that his fleet might return safely to the Tigris and Euphrates. If he could establish the sea route between the Indus and Mesopotamia, he would realize one of his greatest dreams, the knitting together of his empire into a self-sufficient whole.

The next weeks were marked by feverish activity. Alexander explored the whole area of the Delta, often under difficult circumstances, for the local population had a way of vanishing on his approach. The expedition also had to master the phenomenon of ocean tides. Since the Mediterranean is practically tideless, this was their first experience with such things, and in the beginning there was considerable alarm when the tide came in and dashed boats which presumably had been safely beached.

It seems clear that Alexander believed his work would be permanent. He founded cities, constructed dockyards and naval stations. He dredged harbors, laid out citadels. Here was to be the great southeastern terminus of the empire's trade. And since the population was bound to grow, Alexander had irrigation wells dug throughout the countryside.

At the same time, Alexander had to settle the details concerning the last leg of the journey to Mesopotamia. Uppermost in his mind was the safety of the fleet, for the sea route was what mattered above all else. Nearchus would be the admiral, and an excellent one, but there was the problem of supplies. Alexander decided that his own role should be to march along the shore, dig wells and lay down depots of food for Nearchus. In his own account of the expedition, Nearchus says that Alexander had been told that the march ahead was difficult—hardly a novelty for any of his marches—but that no one had any idea of its true dimensions.

Alexander left the Delta in September, 325 B.C., a month ahead of Nearchus, for he hoped to have all the admiral's supplies laid out well in advance. Immediately, however, the temporary character of the work in the Delta became clear. With Alexander gone, the Indians grew bold and threatening, and Nearchus had to leave before the October trade winds—the northeast monsoon—set in. As a result, he was becalmed for several weeks near the mouth of the Indus, but at last he set sail for the Persian Gulf with a fleet of perhaps 150 ships and some 5,000 sailors and marines.

The troops detailed to Nearchus and Craterus enabled Alexander to march with as small an army as possible, approximately 15,000 men. In addition, there were the usual camp followers, traders, scientists, women and children. Although a march across the torrid wastes of Gedrosia (southern Baluchistan) lay ahead, Alexander was able in the beginning to follow the shore, dig wells, and lay down provisions of food as planned. He even founded another Alexandria and arranged for the government of the area. The Phoenician traders with him eagerly collected strange desert plants, especially the gum of myrrh bushes, which they loaded on their mules.

Soon, however, Alexander's own supplies began to run out. The soldiers broke the seals and ate the food, and there was nothing he could do except forgive them. Then he came to the Taloi mountains, whose existence he had not even suspected. This barren range forced him to abandon the coast and all hope of supplying Nearchus.

Two hundred miles of practically waterless desert stretched ahead. The guides lost the way, and the heat was so intense that the army usually had to march at night. Alexander himself did all he could to buoy the spirits of the men: he marched on foot, and whenever a little water was brought especially to him, he poured it into the sand for all to see. He pretended not to notice when the soldiers killed the pack animals and ate their flesh. The troops then knocked the baggage wagons to pieces, since it was too difficult to drag them through the sand, and this, too, cut down on the limited supplies. Soldiers who were taken sick had to be left behind to die.

There seemed to be no end to Alexander's troubles. There was a cloudburst one night, while he and his troops were bivouacked beside a brook, and such a torrent resulted that it drowned many of the wives and children of the camp followers and swept away Alexander's remaining pack animals and baggage. At last, however, they came to the sea, where they obtained water regularly by scraping away the shingle on the beach. Refreshed, they continued on to Carmania (Kerman). At Gulashkird the satrap met them with supplies. The soldiers had survived the ordeal with relatively few losses, but the mortality among the camp followers had been very high.

It was at Gulashkird that Craterus joined Alexander. His march back from the Indus, by way of the Mulla Pass and Candahar, had been uneventful. Part of the army was now reunited, and that was cause for thanksgiving; time could be taken for the founding of another

Alexandria, too. But what of Nearchus? Would the fleet get through?

Nearchus, too, was having difficulties. The shore along which he sailed was desolate. It contained few supplies and even fewer people. The fleet met some true savages, people still living in the Stone Age, half naked and hairy, with fingernails that looked like the claws of beasts. The food of these Fisheaters (as they were called) was fish that they caught in the ebbing tide, or in palm nets. They either ate the fish raw or dried them in the sun and made meal of them. They built their houses of fish bones, the more prosperous among them using the bones of whales that they found cast upon the beach. Their only weapons were wooden spears. When they first saw Nearchus, they thought they could beat him off, but they quickly changed their minds when the catapults on shipboard let loose a shower of missiles.

There were moments when the fleet ran out of food. More terrifying was the time they met a school of whales, spouting mountains of water. Nearchus arranged his ships as though for a sea battle, the trumpets sounded, the men shouted, and then charged. The whales dived in fright, and the men sang the praises of their bold and wise admiral. On another occasion the fleet came to an island, which the pilots said was sacred to the Sun; anyone who landed on it would vanish, they explained. In his practical Greek way, which amounted almost to arrogance, Nearchus went ashore and proved the story a myth.

Nearchus reached the entrance to the Persian Gulf

eighty days after his departure from the Indus. He had lost only four ships. He landed at Harmozia and finally found Alexander at Gulashkird. Alexander was overjoyed by the news of the fleet's safe arrival. He offered sacrifices of thanksgiving to Poseidon and all the gods of the sea, to Heracles, to Apollo the Averter of Evil, and to Zeus the Savior. Processions were held; musical and gymnastic contests were performed. Legend later turned this natural celebration into a Dionysiac orgy. Whatever it was, the immense fact remains that Alexander had made one of the greatest military marches in history, Nearchus had explored an unknown coast and established a sea route between East and West, and Craterus had arrived safely.

The celebrations concluded, Nearchus and the fleet sailed on to the Tigris. Alexander and Hephaestion brought the army in two columns to Persis (early 324 B.C.), almost exactly six years after their first entry and certainly with at least as much pride and joy and sense of power.

XIII

ALEXANDER'S DEATH

THE condition of Cyrus'
tomb at Pasargadae, the ancient capital of Persia, was
symptomatic of the imperial problems awaiting Alexander's return. Someone had rifled the tomb, in spite of
the inscription over its doorway: "O man, whoever you
are, and wherever you come from (for I know you will
come), I am Cyrus, the founder of the Persian Empire. Do
not begrudge me this little earth which covers my body."
The words touched Alexander deeply, for they reminded
him of the uncertainty of human affairs. He put the re-
pair of the tomb in the hands of Aristobulus, the engineer
whose memoirs of the expedition became a major source
of Arrian's history.

The problems facing Alexander were many and varied.

Few people had expected that he would return from India alive, and as a consequence, the empire was in great disorder. Harpalus, the boyhood friend whom Alexander had left at Ecbatana as Imperial Treasurer, had absconded to Greece with a vast fortune. The financial superintendent in Egypt was guilty of several outrages. The Greek and Macedonian colonists in Bactria, despairing of ever seeing home again, were on the verge of revolt; Philip, the satrap in India, had been murdered. The satraps of several other provinces and a number of generals accused one another, or were accused by the people, of various crimes. Alexander ordered the execution of many of these high officials.

This brings us up against an almost insoluble problem, and yet our final estimate of Alexander depends in part on our ability to resolve it. Some of these officials were guilty of the charges brought against them, and there can be little doubt about the justice of their punishment. But the evidence is not clear concerning all of them; in fact, it is practically certain that innocent men were executed, in which case Alexander was himself guilty of a great crime. It is this that we have chiefly in mind when we say that his temper was Alexander's greatest enemy, and that his last years exhibit a growing megalomania, or delusion of grandeur.

It is true that Alexander was almost miraculously alive; he had conquered brilliantly and savagely, and had survived the ordeal of the westward march. At the same time, he was determined to establish an entirely new type of imperialism or, it might be more exact to say, a new way of life for humanity. And yet, on his return to Persia, he found that many high officials—Greeks, Macedonians, and barbarians—had betrayed his trust and, in their eagerness to play the role of petty princes, had done their best to destroy the fabric of his empire. Alexander characteristically decided to put things in order again and at once, with the result that his heavy hand fell on the innocent and the guilty alike.

In the last analysis, deep down, his men still adored him, as we shall have the opportunity to see, but from this point onward they very particularly feared and resented him, too. Their contradictory emotions were only a reflection of Alexander's own contradictions. Whatever the opinion of others might have been about himself, however, Alexander went straight ahead with his work as he conceived it to be.

It was at Susa (spring, 324 B.C.) that Calanus, the Indian philosopher who had joined Alexander long ago, announced that he wished to die. For the first time in his life, he said, he was ill, and he now asked Alexander to build his funeral pyre. Alexander found it impossible to make him change his mind and ordered everything to be prepared. On the appointed day, Alexander arranged a procession of horses and men in full armor. Some people carried incense, others gold and silver cups. Calanus himself was borne in a litter, crowned with garlands in Indian fashion. The Indians in his entourage sang hymns to the gods. When the procession reached the pyre, Calanus told the Macedonians to have a day of feasting, but to Alexander he said ominously, as people liked to relate afterward, "I'll see you soon again at Babylon."

Then Calanus mounted his funeral pyre and ordered it to be lit. The bugles blew, the army raised the battle cry, and the elephants added their shrill notes. As the flames enveloped Calanus, nobody saw him flinch.

A state banquet was also arranged at Susa, in order to dramatize and further Alexander's dream of the fusion of races. He had already expressed himself on the subject at Bactra, when he married Roxane, and now he married Barsine, the daughter of Darius, as well. This served, of course, to legitimize his own position, and in the hope that his children and Hephaestion's might be cousins, he gave Hephaestion Drypetis, another daughter of Darius. Seleucus, whose descendants were to rule Asia for centuries, married Apama, the daughter of Alexander's redoubtable Sogdian opponent, Spitamenes. In all, eighty of Alexander's officers married noble "barbarians."

The weddings were celebrated in Persian fashion, with seats placed in a row for the bridegrooms. After the banquet, the brides came in and sat down next to their husbands. Then each groom, starting with Alexander, took his bride by the right hand and kissed her. Alexander gave dowries to the newly married couples, and he also gave presents to the Greek and Macedonian soldiers who, during all these years, had attached themselves more or less permanently to a foreign woman. These proved to be over ten thousand in number.

Alexander's informal friendliness and comradeship at

this time won him great popularity, and he thought it an opportune moment to pay the debts of his soldiers. The men did not wholly trust him, however, and suspected that he was trying to find out who was dissatisfied with his pay. When this was reported to him, Alexander ordered that the debts should be paid without recording any names.

This also seemed the proper moment to attend to other matters of varying importance: those who had distinguished themselves in one way or another, such as Nearchus, were rewarded; Hephaestion was officially recognized as the second most powerful man in the empire and was given the Persian title of Grand Vizier.

At this time Alexander also resolved a crisis that was threatening Greece. There had always been political exiles in that country, but Antipater, the Macedonian regent, had added to their normal number by setting up tyrannies in various Greek cities and banishing local democrats. The result was that twenty thousand ambitious men swarmed over Greece, a menace to society. By a stroke of the pen, Alexander ordered their return to their home cities. He had no legal right to do this, but apparently public order took precedence in his mind over a body of imperial law that had still to be worked out in detail.

It would be absurd to expect the functioning of a long-established regime at this time, or of normal reactions to it. Alexander's return from India made certain the birth of a new world; outstanding problems had to be solved somehow; and if his further plans were unknown to peo-

ple in general, the best thing for them to do was to play it
safe by all means. That is why, at the Olympic Games
that autumn, the Greeks on their own initiative decided
to deify Alexander. Nor was it long before Greek envoys,
with crowns on their own heads, arrived and crowned
Alexander with golden crowns as if he were a god. The
Greeks were the last people in the world who would have
to be told how to hail the Conqueror of India.

If people did not know exactly what the future held
for them—a question Alexander himself could not have
answered—at least they knew that they were living in a
new day. The official stamp of approval had been placed
on interracial marriage for those who wished it; the new
foundations emphasized Greek culture; Alexander's Persian dress proved that he intended to be more than a
national king; thousands of barbarians were being used in
administration, both in high and small positions; and
the army was composed of various races. Perceptive individuals could see that this added up to a new attitude,
to a dream of universalism—with everyone subject, however, to Alexander's rule.

New ideas, in increasing number and variety, came
with bewildering rapidity. Most people could not grasp
their full meaning, and so they resented them. For example, the arrival of thirty thousand Bactrian youths
who, on Alexander's orders, had been trained in Macedonian fashion, convinced the Macedonians that Alexander was planning to get along without themselves. They
began to yearn openly for the good old days when they

had had a true Macedonian king, such as Philip, and not much later they mutinied at Opis on the Tigris.

The immediate occasion was Alexander's announcement that he was planning to send home with rich presents all those who could no longer serve in the army, either because of wounds or age. Justin, in his historical account, says that the young men in the army insisted that they too be allowed to go home. The Macedonians had angrily mutinied, all of them.

Alexander ordered the ringleaders arrested, and then mounted a platform and addressed the rest. He explained how he and Philip had raised them from their simple origins to the point where they had mastered first Greece and then Asia. Now, if they liked, they could go home and report how they had abandoned their king in Asia, handing him over to the protection of conquered foreigners. "Perhaps," he concluded, "this report of yours will be glorious among men and pious in the eyes of the gods. Depart!"

When he had finished speaking, Alexander shut himself up in his tent for two days and then began to create a Persian army. It was too much for the Macedonians. They and their king might have their differences, but the bond between them was too strong to be broken. They came to his tent and begged his forgiveness. The real trouble, they started to explain, was that he had made Persians his kinsmen. Alexander interrupted and said, "I make all of you my kinsmen." The reconciliation was moving and was sealed by a banquet for no less than nine thousand persons.

Greeks and Macedonians, Medes, Persians, and those of other nationalities sat at Alexander's own table. After dinner, they dipped wine from a large mixing bowl and, when a bugle blew, the entire company made a libation together. Alexander then prayed for partnership in the empire and for unity and concord in a joint commonwealth where all peoples were to be partners rather than subjects. Sir William Tarn, an English historian, has pointed out that this great prayer marks a revolution in human thought, for it was nothing less than a dream of peace and union between Greek and barbarian (expressed, however, at a moment when Alexander was preparing a large army).

The peace and unity of which Alexander spoke were more than a dream. They were founded on acts dating as far back as the days in Asia Minor, when barbarians had been made satraps. They had culminated in Bactria, by which time all of Alexander's fundamental policies had been evolved. It is not for us as historians to guess whether these policies, dramatically proclaimed at the conclusion of large conquest, would eventually have prevailed over Alexander's autocratic rule. But we can point to certain immense facts of history which his life, despite its brevity, made certain. The idea of the *oecumene,* the "inhabited world," had come to stay, a happy counterweight to Aristotle's narrow view of humanity; European rule had taken over Egypt and much of Asia; and a wide prosperity was in the making. Moreover, if Alexander had lived, peace would surely have descended on at least the main areas of his vast empire, perhaps for a long period to come.

The unpleasant, autocratic, and brutal side of Alexander was never more evident, however, than when Hephaestion died at Ecbatana that autumn. Grief for a dear friend was one thing; but Alexander carried it to fantastically enormous lengths. Hephaestion was to be honored as a hero, his cavalry squadron was always to bear his name, a funeral pyre costing thousands of talents was to be erected at Babylon, and thousands of competitors were to take part in the gymnastic and musical contests in his memory. Then Alexander angrily worked off his sorrow by slaughtering a nearby tribe of annoying brigands.

In the spring of 323 B.C. Alexander returned to Babylon, which he planned to make the capital of his empire. All kinds of omens pointing to his death were noticed then or reported later. Nonetheless, he immediately applied himself to a variety of things. He sailed up and down the canals of the Euphrates, as he had those of the Tigris the previous year, removing obstructions to navigation and irrigation. He set aside large sums of money for public works and the support of artists and musicians. Babylon was to be turned into an immense harbor. Alexander also planned to exploit India's mineral wealth, as if there were no doubt about that country's allegiance to him.

At the same time Alexander sent an exploring expedition to the Caspian Sea to determine its relation to Ocean. He founded cities at the head of the Persian Gulf, and made plans to colonize the Gulf's shores. Above all, he planned to discover the size of Arabia and to establish the sea route to Egypt. He organized various expeditions for the circumnavigation of Arabia, some to go down the Persian Gulf and others to sail down the Red Sea from Egypt. Once the connection with Egypt had been made, direct communication between Egypt and India would follow. Nearchus was to be in general charge; and after that, there would be other expeditions, or conquests, as they should more realistically be called.

It is admittedly one of the great "ifs" of history, but it seems clear from the evidence that if Alexander had lived, he would have devoted continuing thought to further exploration and conquest. Inevitably this would have been at the cost of refining the administration of the empire, which at the moment was in many essentials a mere reflection of the Persian. If he really meant it when he said that men should consider the whole inhabited earth as their fatherland, if he was in earnest when he pledged a reign of justice, then the time had arrived for him to give government his undivided attention.

For Alexander, planning and conferences were the new order of the day. These followed immediately, of course, on long marches and fighting. There was apparently to be no relief from incessant physical and mental activity, and Alexander needed rest to recover completely from his wounds. And so, when a fever struck him, he could not throw it off.

The Royal Journal gives a day by day account of Alexander's last illness at Babylon. In its simple and direct language it tells how Alexander sacrificed every day and met with Nearchus and other officers to discuss the Arabian expedition. As his fever worsened, the soldiers forced their way into his palace for a final look at him. Alexander could not speak, but he greeted them by a wave of the hand. "Two days later, toward evening," the Journal concludes, "Alexander died, for that was best." It was June 10, 323 B.C. Alexander the Great was not yet thirty-three years old, and he had reigned twelve years and eight months. The world he left was never again to be the same as it had been.

The army was stunned by Alexander's death. All too quickly, however, the generals began to maneuver for their personal advantage and especially for the prestige of possessing Alexander's body. Thus an entire year passed before the funeral train began its long journey from Babylon to Damascus and Egypt, where at last the great Conqueror was laid to rest in his own city, Alexandria.

Since no general proved strong enough to hold the empire together, it soon broke into three kingdoms along rather natural frontiers: the central core in Macedonia remained; one of Alexander's generals, Seleucus, took Asia, whereupon India promptly fell away; another general, Alexander's biographer Ptolemy, took Egypt. Many of the inhabitants of the new kingdoms, as well as the rulers, were Greeks and Macedonians. The slight differences between the two people were soon forgotten.

This was largely the political situation for the next three centuries, until Rome rounded out her own empire by conquering them all. For centuries afterward Alexander's world continued to be ruled along Western lines.

One of the marked characteristics of the new period, as we have said, was the widespread adoption of Greek civilization, Hellenism, as a common culture. That is why this period is spoken of as the Hellenistic Age. People in Asia and Egypt, if they were ambitious to rise in government or business, learned Greek in addition to their own language, took on Greek ways, Greek thought and art and law. More or less the same influences were reaching Rome; and when that giant of the West conquered the Hellenistic East and incorporated it in its Empire, most of the civilized world had one common culture. (The Far East was too distant to count for much in classical thought.) This explains, for example, why Jesus' Apostles, who spoke a Semitic tongue, wrote the *New Testament* in Greek. It was the common language of the day, and they wanted as many people as possible to receive their message.

We ourselves would feel far more at home in the Hellenistic Age than in Periclean Athens with its high standards of taste, its responsibility, and intensity of life. The culture of the new day was not homogeneous, but was affected both by close contact with foreign civilizations and by the rapid rise of the ordinary man. It is the very modernity of the Hellenistic Age that immediately strikes us. The complexities and contradictions to which we are accustomed were conspicuously present. Science and superstition existed side by side, as did luxury and poverty. New trade routes, immense new cities—such as Alexandria in Egypt, Antioch in northern Syria, Seleucia on the Tigris—meant increased trade, mass production, great wealth, and the constant threat of social revolution. A cosmopolitan population, intent chiefly on pleasure and money-making, gathered in these cities, but people also moved about a good deal. Their diverse ideas and customs merged to the point where culture supplanted race as the thing that mattered most.

New roads were built and policed; harbors were improved; desert routes were provided with wells. One school of philosophers, the Cynics, advised, "Make the world your city." The idea of the "inhabited world" was accepted, and with it there developed (until the coming of Rome) an increased emphasis on arbitration in place of war; and when war broke out, as it often did, it was marked by a growing humanity.

The Hellenistic world constituted a single culture-sphere. It was this less refined and in some ways more vital culture, rather than that of democratic Athens, that civilized Rome and facilitated her creation of a world state and Christianity's ultimate conquest of that state. As such, it is Alexander's monument.

Only the immense force of a great man could produce so sharp a break with the past and set humanity off in a new direction. The actual personality of Alexander, however, was soon buried in an amazing body of literature that came to be called the Alexander Romance, and was supposed to have been written by Callisthenes. It has nothing to do with history, but it does illustrate the extraordinary impression Alexander made on the world. Few stories have been so widely read as these legends, which circulated in twenty-four languages from Iceland to

Malaya. The Orient has always thought of Alexander in the terms of the Romance; the chiefs of certain areas have descended from him, as the common people have descended from his soldiers, and the horses from Bucephalus.

Alexander—or Iskander, as he is more commonly called—appears as the Lord of the Two Horns in the Koran, as a Christian saint in Ethiopia, and as a knight in medieval France. Lands whose existence he could not even have guessed, knew him. His name was spoken on the Blue Nile and in Britain, under the Great Wall of China, and in the Arctic Circle. After he had traveled the entire earth in legend, the Romance brought him to the heavens and, even farther, to the Well of Life; and then, after a descent in a diving bell to the bottom of the sea where the fish paid him homage, he went back to Babylon, only to die of poison.

Such, then, was Alexander's impress on the world for centuries, though the monument of the Hellenistic Age is somewhat more enduring! As for the man himself, crimes, savage fighting, the genius of brilliant generalship, and autocratic rule do indeed mark the road he traveled in attempting to achieve his goal of world government; but in his planning for peace he constantly exhibited intellectual genius and the capacity to grow. Franklin D. Roosevelt once recalled Dante's remark that the sins of the warm-hearted and the sins of the cold-blooded will be weighed in different scales. Taking Alexander's sins and virtues together, the outstanding fact of his life—full of promise for the immediate future, had he lived—was his ability to evolve, from a narrow inheritance, the idea of universalism and cooperation between peoples.

The great Macedonian's dream is of first importance, because history loudly proclaims that ideas, once they have been given voice, will surely be picked up by other men and developed by them. Alexander's idea, or dream, of the solidarity of the world, for example, soon inspired the Stoic school of philosophy to preach the brotherhood of man. And eventually it found its finest expression in Saint Paul's stirring vision of a world in which there shall be "neither Greek nor Jew, barbarian nor Scythian, bond nor free." Since we ourselves have not yet fully realized Alexander's dream, may we not speak of it as his standing challenge to all posterity?

CHRONOLOGICAL SUMMARY OF THE PRINCIPAL EVENTS IN ALEXANDER'S LIFE

356 B.C.   Alexander born at Pella, capital of Macedonia.

338 B.C.   Philip and Alexander defeat the Greeks at Chaeronea.

336 B.C.   Philip murdered. Alexander becomes King of Macedonia.

334 B.C.   Departure for Asia. Battle of the Granicus.

333 B.C.   Battle of Issus.

332 B.C.   Capture of Tyre. Arrival in Egypt.

331 B.C.   Departure from Egypt. Battle of Gaugamela.

330 B.C.   Arrival at Persepolis. Death of Darius.

329–327 B.C.   Campaign in Bactria-Sogdiana.

326 B.C.   Crossing of the Indus. Battle of the Hydaspes. Voyage down the Indus river system.

325 B.C.   Arrival at the Indian Ocean. Departure west-
            ward, Alexander by land, Nearchus by
            sea.

324 B.C.   Return to Persepolis.

323 B.C.   Alexander dies at Babylon on the evening of
            June 10.

INDEX